A HOUSE DIVIDED

Engaging the Issues
through the Politics of Compassion

MARK FELDMEIR

**chalice
press**

Saint Louis, Missouri

An imprint of Christian Board of Publication

Bible quotations, unless otherwise noted, are from the *New Revised Standard Version Bible,* copyright 1989, Division of Christian Education of the National Council of the Churches of Christ in the United States of America. Used by permission. All rights reserved.

ChalicePress.com

Print: 9780827200968

EPUB: 9780827200975

EPDF: 9780827200982

Printed in the United States of America

*Dedicated to the people of
St. Andrew United Methodist Church,
Highlands Ranch, Colorado*

And if a house is divided against itself,
that house will not be able to stand.

(Mark 3:25, NRSV)

Contents

Introduction

If you've grown weary of the hyper-partisanship that plagues and paralyzes our national debate; if you're exhausted by the "outrage industrial complex" that vilifies those on the other side of the political aisle; if you're exasperated by our current culture of divisiveness that turns friends and family members into enemies and makes political progress impossible—there is a more hopeful, generous, and faithful alternative.

It's not a politics of contempt that asserts the righteousness of one's viewpoint while condemning that of the other—as though there is only one way to see a particular issue.

It's not a politics of compromise that seeks to "meet in the middle" and remain there—as though the middle is the only safe, neutral, and civilized space where we can avoid disagreement and all get along.

It's not a politics of moderation that prizes greater ideological unity at the expense of one's personal convictions and values.

It's a politics of compassion that fosters a society grounded in universal concern, care, and commitment to the common good.

A politics of compassion is rooted in Hebrew and Christian Scriptures, along with centuries of Christian tradition, our personal and collective faith experience, and an honest understanding of the societal sins of our past. Taken together, they can help us restore our commonality, reclaim our shared values, and resolve some of the most contentious issues of our day, regardless of our partisan loyalties.

Max Harris and Philip McKibbin's 2015 online essay "The Politics of Love"[1] articulated a values-based politics as a means to call people to think about common values instead of partisan divisions. Harris and McKibbin considered whether instead of a politics of division, we could somehow foster a politics of love — a way of relating to people and responding to real human issues that emphasizes universal care, concern, and commitment fueled by creativity and collaboration. Rather than a "warm feeling" or an emotion that devalues intellectual engagement and honest debate, for these authors love is a motivating ideal that insists we work together for the benefit of the common good, guided by the values of mutuality, respect, and trust. "If love involves a concern for people," they write, "then a politics of love will move this world to a better place for everyone... In such a politics, love would be woven through all of our policy. Embracing a politics of love would change how we justify policy, as well as how we talk about it."

The notion that love might influence politics is not new. It's a foundational ethic intrinsic to all three Abrahamic faiths—Judaism, Islam, and Christianity—and most notably for us to Christianity, where it constitutes the central theme of Jesus of Nazareth's message in the synoptic gospels.

For Jesus, a politics of love manifests itself in the form of compassion, which in Latin means literally to "suffer with another." Genuine compassion evokes a deep concern for the suffering and well-being of neighbor, and is expressed most fully in the "basileia tou theou," the Kingdom of God. Life lived in the Kingdom of God, according to Jesus, is a matter of choosing an alternative to the self-interested values that dominate the society in which one lives, and establishing patterns of relationship with others that are rooted in three core commitments: kinship, kenosis (self-emptying or self-giving), and delight.

Kinship: Jesus created a new kind of family that transcended patrilineal bloodlines, tribes, social ranking, religious purity, and orthodoxy in favor of intimacy, boundless compassion, a shared commitment to the common good, and a deep sense of belonging.

---

[1] https://theaotearoaproject.wordpress.com/2015/05/20/the-politics-of-love-max-harris-and-philip-mckibbin/

Jesus introduced a radically inclusive form of table fellowship in which sinners, tax collectors, enemies, prostitutes, those deemed ritually unclean, the poor, and the dispossessed could sit beside Pharisees, Roman officers, those deemed ritually pure, the powerful, and the wealthy. He called his followers to leave behind their familial, tribal, political, and religious loyalties rooted in exclusion and domination to form a new community rooted in compassion, mercy, and equality.

Kenosis: Jesus expanded the traditional understanding of holiness to include not only personal piety in relationship to God, but also a self-giving, self-emptying solidarity with the poor, the powerless, and the marginalized. Such solidarity freely and willingly surrenders the egoic self, loves and serves others unconditionally, and embraces a commitment to forgiveness and to non-violent, non-coercive means of redemption. In Jesus, the power of voluntary, sacrificial love replaced the competition, exploitation, and scapegoating that is often exercised by those in positions of power and privilege. The same God who poured out God's self to create the cosmos and everything in it was most fully incarnate in Jesus of Nazareth, who called his disciples to pour themselves out freely in sacrificial love for all—especially for the least of God's creation.

Delight: Jesus embodied a way of living in this world that saw the Imago Dei—the image of God—in all living things, and therefore found deep joy simply in being with others and with creation in ways that defied the transactional, reciprocal modes of relationship in which we often relate to one another. Jesus not only liked to party with friends; he was often the very life of the party, transforming the people of his community from a "collection of objects" into a "communion of subjects," as the Catholic theologian Thomas Berry has noted. Jesus called his followers to delight in the dignity and sacred worth of all persons, in all stages of life: children, widows, orphans, sinners, the sick, the demon-possessed, the outcast, and the dying.

In the heart of the Roman Empire, an empire rooted in the values of fear, power, self-interest, domination, and exploitation, the Jesus movement planted alternative communities of diverse people who, empowered by the Spirit, practiced a politics of compassion devoted to kinship, kenosis, and delight, fostering a culture of universal care, concern, and commitment to neighbor that was fueled by extraordinary creativity and collaboration. It was their steadfast devotion to this politics of compassion that ultimately dismantled the unjust systems of the Roman Empire and led to a more just, generous, and caring society.

What might this politics of compassion look like if applied to the most contentious issues of our day? How might it shape our understanding of, and advocacy for, public policy on these issues? How might it inform our everyday conversations with those with whom we disagree politically?

In the pages that follow, we will explore eight of the most divisive issues of our day through the lens of a politics of compassion, seeking to identify those shared values that affirm our commonality and inspire a more creative and collaborative approach to finding solutions and healing our divisions. These issues are climate change, racism, immigration, healthcare, medical aid in dying, Islamic extremism, homosexuality, and the epidemic of social isolation leading to suicide.

In each chapter I propose a set of axioms upon which we can find common ground as Christians, regardless of our partisan loyalties, to help us navigate each of these contentious issues. An axiom is a statement that is taken to be true, and in this case it serves as a premise or starting point for further reasoning. The word comes from the Greek, "axíōma" (ἀξίωμα), which means "that which is thought worthy or evident." An axiom is a statement that is so evident or well established that it is accepted without controversy or question. Examples of an axiom might include: the sun rises in the East; humans have one brain; cats always land on their feet; David Hasselhoff can't sing. Some of the axioms that follow may be more self-evident than others, but *the objective is to reclaim our shared values as people of faith*, so that we can reorder our everyday conversations and renew our commitment to practicing a politics of compassion in ways that embody grace, reason, humility, and universal concern.

To that end, each chapter also includes a study guide for group and individual use. I encourage you to gather together with family and friends, church members, neighbors, and colleagues from both sides of the aisle for courageous and compassionate conversations that model the values outlined throughout this book.

This book is the product of a sermon series I preached at St. Andrew United Methodist Church, a vibrant, politically diverse congregation located in South Denver, CO. The people of St. Andrew are deeply committed to kinship, kenosis, and delight as they seek to bridge the partisan divisions among us through a politics of compassion. The people of St. Andrew have inspired and informed the pages that follow, and so I dedicate this book to them, and to their witness in our community.

Mark Feldmeir

February 14, 2020

1

Climate Change

"God saw everything that he had made, and indeed, it was
very good."
~ Genesis 1:31

On February 14, 1990, the spacecraft Voyager 1 left our planetary
neighborhood for the outer fringes of the solar system. As it reached
a distance of about four billion miles from Earth, engineers briefly
turned the spacecraft around to capture a portrait of our now far-
flung planet. The portrait caught Earth in the center of scattered
light rays—a result of taking the picture so near to the Sun. It
appeared as a tiny, nearly invisible point of light in a vast cosmic
arena, a crescent only 0.12 pixels in size.

Reflecting later on that infinitesimal, almost imperceptible image
of "the pale blue dot," the renowned astronomer, Carl Sagan,
wrote,

> Our posturings, our imagined self-importance, the delusion
> that we have some privileged position in the Universe,
> are challenged by this point of pale light. Our planet is a
> lonely speck in the great enveloping cosmic dark. In our
> obscurity, in all this vastness, there is no hint that help will
> come from elsewhere to save us from ourselves.... There is

perhaps no better demonstration of the folly of human conceits than this distant image of our tiny world. To me, it underscores our responsibility to deal more kindly with one another, and to preserve and cherish the pale blue dot, the only home we've ever known.[1]

Any honest conversation about climate change and the stewardship of the earth must begin by contrasting this sobering, startling image of the pale blue dot with the folly and arrogance of our imperfect ideological viewpoints. By doing so, we stand in humility with the Psalmist who wrote,

> When I look at your heavens, the work of your fingers,
>   the moon and the stars that you have established;
> what are human beings that you are mindful of them,
>   mortals that you care for them? (Ps. 8:3–4)

Our guiding question throughout this book is what Scripture, Christian tradition, and our experience and understanding of God have anything to say about the divisive issues of our time. In this work of Christian ethics, we apply ultimate meaning to proximate concerns in order to inform how we might live more faithfully and responsibly in our world. Guiding this work of Christian ethics are our shared values that together fuel a politics of love and compassion: universal care, infinite concern, and a boundless commitment to all life. Embracing a politics of love affects how we form and justify our positions and policies on complex social issues, as well as the manner in which we talk about them.

We know that the majority of Americans perceive climate change as an urgent social concern.[2] According to a January 2020 survey conducted by the Yale Program on Climate Change Communication and George Mason University's Center for Climate Change Communication, the proportion of Americans who are "alarmed" by global warming tripled over the last five years and is now at an all-time high. Almost six in ten Americans

---

[1]Excerpt from Carl Sagan, *Pale Blue Dot* (New York: Random House, 1994), quoted at http://www.planetary.org/explore/space-topics/earth/pale-blue-dot.html

[2]https://news.gallup.com/poll/244367/top-issues-voters-healthcare-economy-immigration.aspx

are either "alarmed" or "concerned" by global warming, signifying a major shift in public perception of the issue."[3]

If the majority of Americans are concerned about climate change, then why is the issue so contentious in our political debate?

Since the early 20th century, temperatures on earth have increased approximately 1.8°F. Over this same period, atmospheric levels of greenhouse gases such as carbon dioxide (CO_2) and methane (CH_4) have increased measurably, and sea levels have risen progressively. Both sides in the climate change debate agree on these points.

But those on one side of the debate argue that rising levels of atmospheric greenhouse gases are a direct result of human activities such as burning fossil fuels, that the rate of increase in CO_2 gasses is speeding up, and that these increases are causing severe climate changes, including global warming, loss of sea ice, rising sea levels, stronger storms, and more droughts. They contend that immediate action is necessary to reduce greenhouse gas emissions and to prevent dire climate changes, and they point to the overwhelming consensus among climate scientists who support this view.

Those on the other side of the debate argue that human-generated greenhouse gas emissions are too small to change the earth's climate substantially, and that the planet is capable of absorbing those increases. They contend that Earth's climate has always warmed and cooled, and that warming over the 20th century was primarily the result of natural processes such as fluctuations in the sun's heat and in the trajectory of ocean currents. They assert that the theory of human-caused global climate change is based on questionable measurements, faulty climate models, and misleading science, and they point to the more than 1000 climate scientists around the world who support this view.

So, for the majority of Americans, the debate is not about whether the climate is actually changing, but whether human activity is causing or contributing to it, and whether humans can do anything to prevent it.

---

[3]https://www.mercurynews.com/2020/01/17/poll-americans-are-more-concerned-now-about-climate-change/

According to a national poll by The Washington Post and the Kaiser Family Foundation conducted in August 2019, more than three in four U.S. adults and teenagers alike agree that humans are influencing the climate. The overwhelming majority of them said it's not too late for society to come up with solutions, but a third of adults who say humans are causing climate change don't think they can personally make a difference, the poll found.

In November 2018, the *Fourth Annual Climate Assessment*, a congressionally mandated climate assessment report authored by scientists from 13 different agencies, concluded that temperatures in the U.S. are 1.8°F higher than 100 years ago; seas are nine inches higher; heat waves, hurricanes and wildfires are more extreme; and climate change could cut our Gross Domestic Product (GDP) by 10 percent by 2100 if there are no changes. They reported that, "based on extensive evidence, it is extremely likely that human activities, especially emissions of greenhouse gases, are the dominant cause of the observed warming since the mid-20th century. There is no convincing alternative explanation supported by the extent of the observational evidence."[4]

Ben Sasse, the highly regarded Republican senator from Nebraska, said recently, "I think it's clear that the climate is changing. I think reasonable people can differ about how much and how rapidly. But I think it's clear that it's changing and... that humans are a contributing factor."[5]

It is Sasse's emphasis on reasonableness that leads us to our first axiom—a statement that is so evident or well established that it's accepted without controversy. In addressing the issue of climate change, I want to begin not with a theological axiom but with a purely pragmatic one:

Axiom #1: When the cost of error is too high, the wise hedge their bets.

If, for ideological reasons, we cannot agree that human activity

---

[4]https://nca2018.globalchange.gov/downloads/NCA4_2018_FullReport.pdf

[5]https://www.realclearpolitics.com/video/2018/11/25/sen_ben_sasse_on_climate_change_you_have_to_innovate_into_the_future.html

contributes to climate change, then we should consider it pragmatically, through the lens of risk-reward analysis. Even if we cannot prove the veracity of human-caused climate change, the most prudent approach is to act as if it is true. This is because if it is true, the benefits of betting that it's true are enormous. Yes, we incur the cost of self-restraint by altering our lifestyles, but relative to the payoff, which in this case is the survival of human civilization, our cost is pretty low.

By contrast, if human-caused climate change is real and we bet against it, the cost is catastrophic: floods, drought, and international conflicts over water, land, and food could potentially end civilization as we know it. That is an infinite loss.

If we cannot agree that human activity contributes to climate change, then we can at least agree that the consequences of betting against it and being wrong far exceed the consequences of betting on it being true and being wrong.

This simple logic serves as justification for why so many of us purchase life insurance policies. For most people who own life insurance, the likelihood of dying prematurely is extremely low. Most of us will pay out far more money than we'll ever get back. Nevertheless, we still believe in the efficacy of life insurance. We are willing to incur a small cost today to mitigate a potentially enormous cost to our families tomorrow.

In the debate over climate change, does it not make logical sense to take out a life insurance policy on the planet? If there is any chance that the prevailing science is right about climate change, as the vast majority of climate scientists suggest, then we have a moral obligation to do what we can now to prevent it from continuing.

Jesus advocated for such prudence when he told a parable about two men who built houses. One of the men dug deeply and laid the foundation of his house on rock; when a flood arose, the river burst against his house but could not shake it, because it had been well built. Said Jesus, "the one who hears and does not act is like a man who built a house on the ground without a foundation. When the river burst against it, immediately it fell, and great was the ruin of that house" (Luke 6:49).

For Christians, there are more than purely logical, pragmatic reasons for caring for the earth. There are profoundly theological reasons as well, which leads us to our second axiom.

Axiom #2: The act of creation was God's first incarnation.[6]

Christians have always understood Jesus of Nazareth as the physical incarnation of God—the one in whom God dwelled most fully, in flesh and blood, two thousand years ago in Galilee. But that was simply the moment in time when God became human and personal.

According to the creation story in Genesis 1, there was an earlier moment, before time as we know it, when God decided to materialize and the divine spirit took physical form: "In the beginning God created the heavens and the earth. Now the earth was formless and empty, darkness was over the surface of the deep, and the Spirit of God was hovering over the waters" (Genesis 1:1–2). Then the Spirit of God beckoned the formlessness and emptiness to life, and that same Spirit entered into the creation. Suddenly, every living thing became a physical revelation of the invisible nature and character of God: light, water, land, sun, moon, stars, plants, trees, fruit, birds, serpents, cattle, fish, and "every kind of wild beast." According to Genesis 1, you can look at every living thing and see something of the nature, character, and presence of God.

When Christians sing the Sanctus—"Holy, holy, holy... Heaven and earth are full of your glory"—they are affirming this notion that Creation was God's first incarnation, and that the divine spirit dwells in all living things. They are saying that the earth, and all the things of the earth, are infused with God's glory and presence.

If God dwells in all created things, then what we do to any one thing, we do to God. As Kentuckian author Wendell Berry suggests, "There are no unsacred places; there are only sacred places and desecrated places." There is a unity to creation that reflects the

---

[6]Richard Rohr, "Creation as the Body of God," *Radical Grace*, vol. 23, no. 2 (Center for Action and Contemplation: 2010): 3, 22.

unity and fullness of God. Desecration is the disintegration of that sacred unity.

Astronauts returning from space flight often refer to a unique phenomenon called the "overview effect." The phrase was first coined by writer Frank White in 1987 as he was flying across the country in an airplane. Looking out the window, he imagined that anyone living in space would always have an overview. They would be able to see things that we know intellectually, but do not experience personally—namely, that Earth is one system, that we are all part of that system, and that there is a certain unity and coherence to it all.

Astronauts frequently speak of this cognitive shift in awareness that comes from seeing planet Earth in space. They report being overwhelmed and awed by the fragility and unity of all of life. From space, Earth suddenly looks like a tiny, delicate ball of life, hanging in the void, shielded by a paper-thin layer of atmosphere that is its only protection from the deadly ultraviolet radiation of the sun. From space, national boundaries vanish, the international conflicts that divide people become trivial, and the preservation of the earth becomes glaringly urgent. Astronauts who have experienced the "overview effect" describe it as profoundly spiritual and humbling, revealing the oneness of life on Earth and everything essential to its survival.

The NASA astronaut Ron Garan experienced this phenomenon, though he called it by a different name. Clamped into a robotic arm over the International Space Station in 2008, looking down at Earth, he felt as if time stood still. He was flooded with emotion and awareness. He recounts:

> [A]s I looked down at the Earth—this stunning, fragile oasis, this island that has been given to us, and that has protected all life from the harshness of space—a sadness came over me, and I was hit in the gut with an undeniable, sobering contradiction. In spite of the overwhelming beauty of this scene, serious inequity exists on the apparent paradise we have been given. I couldn't help thinking of the nearly one billion people who don't have clean water to drink,

the countless number who go to bed hungry every night, the social injustice, conflicts, and poverty that remain pervasive across the planet.

Seeing Earth from this vantage point gave me a unique perspective—something I've come to call the orbital perspective. Part of this is the realization that we are all traveling together on the planet and that if we all looked at the world from that perspective we would see that nothing is impossible.[7]

This "overview effect" or "orbital perspective" is God's view of God's creation.

Many other humans have described their similar response to the holiness and fragility of the earth. Chief Seattle, the 19th-century Native American leader, described it this way:

Every part of the earth is sacred... Every shining pine needle, every sandy shore, every mist in the dark woods, every clear and humming insect is holy...We are part of the earth and it is part of us. The perfumed flowers are our sisters, the deer, the horse, the great eagle, these are our brothers. The rocky crests, the juices in the meadows, the body heat of the pony, and the man, all belong to the same family.[8]

What we do to the earth, we do to God and to ourselves. All things are connected like a great web of life. The earth connects us to God, and it connects us to one another. This leads us to our final axiom:

Axiom #3: We have lost our intimate connection with creation.

We can conveniently point to legislation as a solution to human-caused climate change, but the real solution begins with shared commitment to a more intimate relationship with creation. It begins with a return to the deep connection humans once had to the earth but abandoned in the modern world when we chose

---

[7]https://www.space.com/28838-orbital-perspective-book-excerpt.html
[8]https://www.savethefrogs.com/d/students/chief-seattle.html

domination of the earth instead of *dominion* over the earth. For in fact Genesis 1:26 reads as follows: "Then God said, 'Let us make humankind in our image, according to our likeness; and let them have dominion over the fish of the sea, and over the birds of the air, and over the cattle, and over all the wild animals of the earth, and over every creeping thing that creeps upon the earth.'" In short, God gave humans dominion over all that is, but "dominion" is not "domination." Parents exercise dominion over their children when they are young and vulnerable. Dominion connotes a sense of care, compassion, stewardship, and generosity. By contrast, domination suggests exploitation, coercion, and manipulation for self-gain. Compassionate parents would never abuse their children in the name of exercising dominion over them. Caring, responsible parents would never willfully impair their children's potential to thrive as human beings. They would never neglect their children's obvious needs or injuries, or concede that, while their children may be sick, the science is still too inconclusive to seek proper treatment. On the contrary, loving parents would do everything necessary to ensure that their children thrive.

Dominion is not a right, but a responsibility and a holy privilege. When God granted humans dominion over the earth, God expected them to ensure that it would thrive.

But it is difficult to love something that you do not know personally. Recall the creation story in Genesis 2:19–20 that tells of Adam giving every created thing a name: " So out of the ground the LORD God formed every animal of the field and every bird of the air, and brought them to the man to see what he would call them; and whatever the man called every living creature, that was its name. The man gave names to all cattle, and to the birds of the air, and to every animal of the field."

Humanity's first job was to name the birds, the trees, and all the creeping and crawling things. Why did God give humans this important task? Because when you name something, like a child or even a pet, or when you know the name of someone or something, you connect with them. The object becomes a subject.

But in the modern world, most living things are objects to most of us—disconnected from us, disembodied from our community. The earth is simply a machine that produces and gives us what we want. When we "otherize" or objectify any form of life, we are more prone to abuse and exploit it.

Most of us live in concrete and asphalt worlds. We go days, weeks, and even months without ever seeing a stream, a sunset, a falling star, or wildlife. Our children assume that milk comes from grocery stores rather than cows. Our food comes to us preprocessed, and often precooked, so we never see its connection to soil, water, sunlight, and air. We open our tap for fresh water and drink without ever having to pump it from a well or gather it from a stream.

We have become so physically and emotionally detached from the natural world that we have lost a relationship with creation that is essential to our well-being. We fail to see ourselves as part of nature, so we are not personally or emotionally affected by the deterioration of rainforests, rising sea levels, the dwindling numbers of songbirds and insects, the extinction of species, or the loss of coral reefs. We are not particularly alarmed by the signs of climate change, or willing to make personal lifestyle changes because we see the earth as a machine that produces *for our benefit*, rather than as a living organism of which we are simply one part in an eco*system*.

A Christian response to climate change begins with reclaiming the intimate connection humans once had with creation through simple practices such as gardening, animal husbandry, composting, harvesting rainwater, birdwatching, spending more time in nature, and learning more about the indigenous peoples who came before us. These are just a few of the countless ways that we can delight in the natural resources of the earth and reclaim our kinship with creation. But it also requires a commitment to kenosis, or self-giving, through personal lifestyle changes that will benefit creation. If you feel called to make personal lifestyle changes in response to the issue of climate change, these four simple recommendations can have the greatest impact:

- Replace the regular incandescent light bulbs in your home with compact fluorescent light bulbs (CFLs). CFLs use 60 percent less energy than a regular bulb. This simple switch will save about 300 pounds of carbon dioxide a year, per bulb—that's like your weight and my weight together.

- Plant a tree. A single tree will absorb one ton of carbon dioxide over its lifetime. Assuming its lifetime will exceed your own, that tree will also a be gift to the generation that follows you.

- Moderate your red meat consumption. Methane is the second most significant greenhouse gas, and cows are one of the greatest methane emitters. Their grassy diet and multiple stomachs cause them to produce methane, which they exhale with every breath.

- Reduce the number of miles you drive by walking, biking, carpooling, or taking mass transit whenever possible. Reducing your weekly driving by just 10 miles would eliminate about five hundred pounds of carbon dioxide emissions a year.

We stand at the edge of two worlds—the world that God created, and the world that is imperiled by our abuse of it. If you look at the science and still do not know what or whom to believe; or if the problem seems so big that you do not know where to begin, perhaps you can start by imagining some future conversation with your children, or your grandchildren, in which they ask you two simple questions:

When did you *know*? And what did you *do*?

Further Study and Reflection for Groups or Individuals

A Prayer for Guidance and Grace

God of the Universe, God also of the Single Cell, heaven and earth are full of your glory. We gather in awe of all that you have created and called good in the world. In a spirit of humility, we gather with gratitude that in your infinite wisdom and concern for creation, you are ever mindful of us. Amen.

Icebreaker

When was the last time you felt or experienced an intimate connection with creation? Where were you? What was your response?

Why do you think climate change can be such a divisive or contentious issue for Americans?

Do you believe that climate change is a consequence of human activity, a natural cycle of the earth, or both? Why?

What, if any, changes to your lifestyle/energy consumption have you made due to your views on climate change?

Deep Dive

What did you learn in this chapter about the historical trends of climate change, according to the *Fourth Annual Climate Assessment*?[9] Is the government-based science on climate change reliable?

How do the values of our culture interfere with our ability to care for, and connect with, creation?

What are some of the things we could change in the way we live and work to help decrease the amount of CO_2 we emit into the atmosphere? What would you be willing to give up in order to reduce our carbon footprint?

If we cannot agree that human activity contributes to climate change, does it still make sense to consider it pragmatically, through the lens of risk-reward analysis, and "hedge our bets?" If there is any chance that the prevailing science is right about climate change, do we have a moral obligation to do what we can now to prevent it from continuing?

Engaging the Text

Read Genesis 1:26–31.

According to v. 27, "God created humankind in his image." What are some of the qualities or attributes of God's image and character that humans embody? How do these qualities and

---

[9]Available online at https://www.globalchange.gov/nca4.

attributes influence our relationship with creation?

What does it mean to "fill the earth and subdue it; and have dominion over the fish of the sea and over the birds of the air and over every living thing that moves upon the earth" (v. 28)? What is the difference between "dominion" and "domination?"

According to v. 31, "God saw everything that he had made, and indeed, it was very good." Are there forms of life, or aspects of the creation, that are of greater or lesser value to you? Which ones? Why or why not?

Is it possible to maintain a thriving U.S. economy while implementing responsible climate policies that reduce or minimize atmospheric levels of greenhouse gases? If so, how?

Closing Prayer

God of heaven and earth, you desire a reconciliation of the whole creation. Forgive us our selfish and destructive ways. Help us to see your presence and glory in all living things, and to walk humbly on the earth as we seek a life that is more connected to all you have created and called good. Amen.

2

Racism

Then God said, "Let us make humankind in our image,
according to our likeness."
~ Genesis 1:26

Baltimore, Ferguson, Charlottesville, Charleston.
Trevon, Tamir, Sandra, Philando, and Freddie.
Kaepernick, Serena, Barkley, and Lebron.
White supremacy, white privilege, white fragility, and woke.
"Hands up, don't shoot." "I can't breathe." Black Lives Matter.

These are just some of the people, places, controversies, and catchphrases that have come to define the complexities of today's conversation about race in the U.S. Over the last decade, that conversation has changed dramatically. From police shootings to the mass incarceration of African Americans, from the resurgence of white nationalism to "taking a knee" during the National Anthem, many Americans are slowly realizing that a "post-racial America" is a fallacy and that systemic racism rests just beneath the surfaces of our society, institutions, politics, economies, and even churches. Our outrage is easily activated whenever some brazenly racist incident is exhumed for our news feeds. But our brief flashes of indignation over these incidents often conceal our own racism and the racism woven into the fabric of the American way of life in which we all participate.

It's for this reason that a conversation about race can be both contentious and delicate. On the one hand, we know that blatant racism must be called out and resisted whenever we see it. On the other hand, because we participate in social systems that are inherently discriminatory, we know that we are unquestionably implicated at the very least in the more subtle, unconscious expressions of racism. How can we talk about race without the defensiveness, reflexivity, and scapegoating that accompanies such conversations? Is it possible to talk about race with such honesty and daring that we might be implicated, awakened, and transformed?

Our objective throughout this book is to set aside the sound bites, talking points, and caricatures that dominate our political conversations and take up the more important work of Christian ethics. In these pages, we are applying ultimate meaning to proximate concerns by inviting Scripture, Christian tradition, and our personal and collective experience of faith to inform how we think about, and respond to, particular social issues. Our concern is less about how we vote and for whom we cast our vote, and more about why we vote, and how our vote might contribute to a politics of love devoted to the shared values of universal care, concern, and commitment to the common good.

According to a Pew Research Center survey conducted in February 2019, about six in 10 Americans (58 percent) say race relations in the U.S. are bad, and of those, few see them improving. Blacks are particularly gloomy about the country's racial progress. More than eight in 10 black adults say the legacy of slavery affects the position of black people in America today, including 59 percent, who say it affects it a great deal. About eight in 10 blacks (78 percent) say the country hasn't gone far enough when it comes to giving black people equal rights with whites, and fully one half say it's unlikely that the country will ever achieve racial equality.[1]

---

[1]https://www.pewsocialtrends.org/2019/04/09/race-in-america-2019/

Given this widespread pessimism, how do we have honest and hopeful conversations about the complex issue of racism in America? Perhaps it begins by acknowledging our personal limitations and inherent ignorance. As I write this chapter, I am acutely aware of the irony of a relatively comfortable, privileged, white male from the south suburbs of Denver presuming to have something meaningful to say on the issue of race. What do I really know about race relations in America, and what wisdom can I possibly impart, from my limited, white, privileged experience, that will not sound paternalistic or reductionist?

I do not presume to have arrived on the issue, or to be "woke." I simply want to share with you what I have discovered on my own journey toward greater awareness of racism in America, and with my own participation in systems, both visible and hidden, that perpetuate it. I want to begin with two stories that might open us to an honest conversation about this sensitive issue.

The first story is about a colleague who shared with me an experience she had late one night while on a business trip in a major city. She had just finished a long meeting and was walking alone to her car in a dark, mostly empty parking lot. Once inside, she attempted to start her car, only to discover that the battery was dead. There she was, alone, with a car that wouldn't start, in a dark parking lot, stranded in an unfamiliar city past midnight.

As she hunted for her roadside assistance card, she noticed an older model truck driving slowly through the lot. To her it seemed as if the truck was prowling in her general direction. She checked and rechecked the locks on the doors and tried again and again to start the engine. The truck slowly approached and finally came to a stop in front of her car. In the dim light of the parking lot, she could see a tall black man emerge from the truck holding what appeared to be a thick rope. Her heart raced as he walked slowly toward her car. Flushed with fear and panic, she fumbled for her phone and started to dial 911, when suddenly the man knocked on her windshield, held up a pair of jumper cables, and said, "I work maintenance here, ma'am. I noticed earlier that you'd left your headlights on. You don't have to get out of the car. Just pop the hood and I'll help you get it started."

All at once, her fear turned to relief, and then her relief turned to guilt. She wondered why she had been so afraid, and what her fear revealed about her unconscious beliefs and biases.

The second story is told by Dr. Kamau Bobb, who serves on the faculty at Georgia Tech and holds a global leadership position at Google. He was crawling along in rush hour traffic just before dusk, heading home from work, when red and blue lights suddenly flashed behind him. He pulled over, and the officer pulled over behind him. This, said Bobb, "is the singular moment in American life where Black men wish they were White women. This is the moment that drives fear into the hearts of Black people. Anything in the interaction with police can escalate to deadly outcomes... and there was no telling how this would go."

The approaching officer reached the back fender and put his hand on his gun. Bobb was now fearful. He rolled down the window as the officer approached, and that was when he heard the voice: "Put your hands on the steering wheel where I can see them." Bobb reached for his wallet, and again, he was ordered to put his hands on the wheel. Bobb says, "For White people... who typically say that if you've done nothing wrong, everything will be fine, this is the moment they don't understand. This is the terror moment... the moment of anxiety at fever pitch."[2]

After the arrival of another patrol car and several intense minutes of questioning and radio calls, the encounter ended without further escalation. But if you are Kamau Bobb, what do you do with the fear and humiliation of such an experience? Where does it go?

* * *

Throughout this book, I am proposing axioms to help us find common ground and agreement on complex, divisive issues. An axiom is a simple and self-evident statement that serves as a premise or starting point for further reasoning and dialogue.

As we consider the topic of race in America, we begin with what is simple and self-evident:

---

[2]http://kamaubobb.com/2019/01/police-computing-and-nationalism/

Axiom #1: How we think about racism is largely determined by our own particular race.

For my friend stranded in the unlit parking lot, fearing the black man who ultimately came to her aid revealed her unconscious bias based on skin color and stereotypes. For her, and for many whites, racism is commonly understood as prejudicial attitudes and behaviors grounded in a belief that race is the primary determinant of human traits and capacities. My friend is a good person for whom the term "racist" would seem entirely inappropriate. But that sudden awareness of her unconscious bias led to a profound and humbling sense of guilt.

But for Kamau Bobb, ordered to keep his hands on the wheel during a routine traffic stop, racism is more than just prejudicial attitudes and behaviors. He experiences it systemically in the common structures of everyday life that make the world unfair and unsafe for blacks, and that experience leads to a deep and chronic sense of humiliation and fear.

How we think and talk about racism is largely determined by the color of our skin, and our experience of living in that skin. Most whites understand racism primarily as prejudicial attitudes and behaviors. But most blacks experience racism primarily as systemic or systems-wide discrimination and injustice.

The fourth-century theologian Thomas Aquinas phrased this axiom another way: "Whatever is received is received according to the manner of the receiver." Aquinas suggested that we receive and perceive things not as *they* are, but as *we* are. Whatever we communicate to another person can only be received by that person insofar as he or she is able to understand it. This is why it can be so difficult to talk with a tourist from a foreign country, for example, or with a newborn infant, or your Golden Retriever, or your teenager. Whatever is received is received according to the manner of the receiver.

So, what does this mean? It means that if we want to understand racism in the U.S., as uncomfortable as it might be for us, we have the moral responsibility to open our eyes and see our society more truthfully, and to become more receptive to what it is like to be black in the U.S.

Here are some astonishing statistics that may help bring clarity to this conversation:

- Black men are about 2.5 times more likely to be killed by police than are white men.[3]

- If you are black in America, you are six times more likely to be incarcerated than a white person.[4]

- The median black family has only 10.2 percent of the wealth of the median white family.[5]

- Blacks are about 2.5 times as likely to be in poverty as whites.[6]

- The unemployment rate for black workers is consistently about twice as high as it is for white workers.[7]

- The typical black worker makes 82.5 cents on every dollar earned by the typical white worker.[8]

- The homicide rate for blacks between the ages of 10–34 years is 13 times the rate for whites.[9]

- A black child is six times more likely as a white child to have or have had an incarcerated parent.[10]

- Although black children are approximately 16 percent of the child population nationally, they make up 30 percent of the child abuse and neglect fatalities.[11]

All of this begs the question: Are these statistics a consequence of something more systemic than individual prejudice?

---

[3]https://www.prisonpolicy.org/scans/police_mort_open.pdf
[4]https://www.epi.org/publication/50-years-after-the-kerner-commission/?mod=article_inline
[5]Ibid.
[6]Ibid.
[7]Ibid.
[8]Ibid.
[9]https://www.sciencedirect.com/science/article/pii/S07493797183 1907X
[10]https://www.epi.org/publication/mass-incarceration-and-childrens-outcomes/
[11]http://blackchildlegacy.org/resources/child-abuse-and-neglect/

The late writer David Foster Wallace told the story about two young fish that were swimming along when they happened to meet an older fish swimming toward them. The older fish nodded at them and said, "Good morning, boys, how's the water?" The two young fish continued to swim on for a bit, when eventually one of them looked over at the other and asked, "What the heck is water?"[12]

Beyond our individual and often unconscious biases, is there something about the water in which we are swimming, something invisible in the society in which we live, that many who are white do not even see?

How we think and talk about racism is largely determined by the color of our skin and our experience of living in that skin. Acknowledging this simple truth leads us to our second axiom, which echoes the words of the contemporary black writer, Ta-Nehisi Coates:

Axiom #2: "Race is the child of racism, not the father."

History proves that the exploitation of black persons came first, and only then did an ideology of unequal races follow. To make slavery work, we had to create an ideology of exploitation to support it and categories of race to legitimize it. Race is a social concept, not a scientific one.

This is not only historically, but also biblically, true. Genesis 1 takes us back to the very beginning, to the creation story, when Earth was a massive soup of nothingness, a bottomless emptiness, an inky blackness. God's Spirit brooded like a bird above the abyss, giving birth first to light, then sky, land, plants and trees, stars. More life soon followed: fish, cattle, birds, reptiles, bugs, gnats. Then, finally, came God's brightest idea of all: to form a creature not only out of God's own breath or spirit, but in God's own image. God called the creature "human," 'ādām in the Hebrew, which was God's generic term for humankind. God spoke: "Let us make human beings in our image, make them reflecting our nature" (Gen 1:26, *MSG*).

------

[12]https://fs.blog/2012/04/david-foster-wallace-this-is-water/

"In our image, reflecting our nature." Theologians call this the Imago Dei, the image of God, and it expresses the inherent and equal worth of all human beings, which does not recognize distinctions of skin color or race apart from the human race as a whole. People may have different skin color, but they belong to one human race descended from one parentage, all of whom are created in the image of God spiritually, rationally, morally, and bodily.

The idea of race is a fiction—a social construct birthed by a sinful ideology of supremacy called racism. "Race is the child of racism, not the father." It took me a while to get my head around this, but when I did, I finally understood racism as more than personal prejudice based on skin color, but as an ideology that has imbedded itself in systems that have endured for over four hundred years in America.

This leads us to our fourth and final axiom:

Axiom #3: Colorblindness is a myth that blinds us to the truth about racism.

I grew up in the suburbs of Southern California in the 1970s and '80s, in a time and place in which it would have been unacceptable to utter a racial slur or racist comment. It was, as we understood it then, an era of complete racial integration in every aspect of society. Some of my favorite TV shows were "Soul Train," "What's Happening?" and "White Shadow." I believed the cultural narrative that we are all the same and all equal, and that colorblindness was the antidote to racism. I believed in that beautiful dream about a world where people are judged "not by color of their skin but by the content of their character." In Sunday school we sang, "Red and yellow, black and white, all are precious in His sight," while our parents had sung, "We shall overcome." It felt to a lot of white people as if the Civil Rights movement had finally accomplished the goal of a post-racial society.

But it never occurred to me in middle school or later in high school that in my middle-class suburban town there were very few black people. I believed with all my heart that we were all the same. I didn't understand that if that were really true, we would all be living in the same place, sharing the same public spaces.

Only much later in life did I understand, in part, why that was not the case.

On June 22, 1944, the Servicemen's Readjustment Act of 1944, commonly known as the G.I. Bill, was signed into law to help our World War II veterans adjust to civilian life by providing them with benefits, including low-cost mortgages, low-interest loans, and college tuition. It provided a massive infusion of capital for people who, after returning from war, would face extraordinary challenges in making ends meet and carving out a stable future for themselves and their families.

One important provision of the G.I. Bill was low interest, zero down payment home loans for service members, with more favorable terms on loans for new construction. Millions of American families moved out of urban apartments and flooded to the suburbs, and so began the suburbanization of America and the flight from urban centers.

But not everyone went.

Because the G.I. Bill programs were directed by local, white officials, many of our black veterans did not benefit like our white veterans did. Banks and mortgage agencies consistently refused loans to blacks. As millions of veterans went to back to school, only one-fifth of all blacks who applied for educational benefits went to college.

As the American suburbs flourished, our urban centers floundered. School funding was now tied to property taxes, which pulled the economic rug out from underneath inner-city education. Banks stopped giving loans to businesses in impoverished urban centers, a policy known as redlining. Shops on Main Streets were shuttered. Unemployment skyrocketed. And eventually our inner cities collapsed after this tragic game of social Jenga finally played itself out.

For the black community, "we shall overcome" felt a lot like "we've been overcome."

Meanwhile, whites were told that society had made progress on the issue of race, that we were all equal and could get along now. But it wasn't true. And the prophet Jeremiah cries out,

They have treated the wound of my people carelessly,

saying, "Peace, peace,"

when there is no peace (Jeremiah 6:14).

Imagine training for months to run a marathon, only to discover on race day that not all the runners start the race at the same place. In this race, some start at the five-mile marker, others at the 10-mile marker, and still others at the half-way point. When the starting pistol goes off, you're already losing. When you raise your complaint to the race director, you're told that if you'd only worked harder and trained better, you might have improved your position in the pack.

I admit that all of this talk of white privilege touches a tender nerve and sends me into a state of denial or guilt. Robin DiAngelo calls this "white fragility," a state in which even a minimum amount of racial tension becomes intolerable and triggers a range of defensive emotions and behaviors, including the outward display of anger and fear, and behaviors such as argumentation, microaggression, or silence.

A healthy alternative to feeling bad about being white is to know one's history. We can do nothing about our unconscious and unspoken biases unless we know our history. Our well-intentioned colorblindness keeps us blind to our history. When we know our history, we come to see that, in the words of William Faulkner, "The past is never dead. It's not even past."

So, what can we do? Where do we go from here?

Can I offer three suggestions?

First, if you're white, listen to people, especially to people of color, who are willing to share about their experiences of racism. By doing so, you will become a more informed student of history and of place so that you know the stories, experiences, and the collective wounds of the people of color in your community. Such conversations can be uncomfortable and even triggering, but they create opportunities for deeper intimacy, greater understanding, and a sense of kinship grounded in a shared commitment to the common good.

Second, talk to others about what you don't understand about racism, and what you still need to learn. None of us has all the answers. All of us have unconscious biases and beliefs which, when made conscious through our thoughts and actions, lead to feelings of guilt and defensiveness. Kenosis, or self-giving, calls us to surrender the ego and to acknowledge our flaws and limitations. Lean into vulnerable conversations with honesty, courage, and grace for yourself and others.

And finally, where there is opportunity for relationships with people of different races and cultures, enter into them as deeply as the other will permit, with humility, because in the end, it's not right believing (orthodoxy) alone that will heal the racial divisions and wounds in our country, but also right loving (orthopraxis). The fruit of right loving is taking delight in the unique expressions of cultural diversity, including art, music, food, and language.

Further Study and Reflection for Groups or Individuals

A Prayer for Guidance and Grace

God of justice, in your wisdom you create all people in your image, without exception. Through your goodness, open our eyes to see the dignity, beauty, and worth of every human being. Open our minds to understand that all your children are brothers and sisters in the same human family. Open our hearts to repent of racist attitudes, behaviors, and speech that demean others. Open our ears to hear the cries of those wounded by racial discrimination, and their passionate appeals for change. Strengthen our resolve to make amends for past injustices and to right the wrongs of history. And fill us with courage that we might seek to heal wounds, build bridges, forgive and be forgiven, and establish peace and equality for all in our communities. Amen.[13]

Icebreaker

When it comes to racism in the U.S, today, do you believe that the bigger problem is discrimination built into our laws and institutions, or discrimination based on the prejudice of individuals like us?

Do you agree that how we talk about race is largely determined by our own particular race or skin color? How have you experienced racism personally?

What is meant by the phrase, "white privilege?" What about "white fragility?" What emotions or reactions do these phrases stir up for you?

Why do you think race can be such a divisive or contentious issue for Americans?

Deep Dive

If you're not black, what did you learn in this chapter about what it's like to be black in the U.S. today?

Do you agree that "color blindness" is an obstacle to addressing the systemic issue of racism in the U.S.?

What role did the G.I. Bill play in perpetuating institutionalized racism in the second half of the 20th century? Do you believe that the G.I. Bill favored whites over blacks? If so, how? And why?

How well informed are you about the history of racism in your own city or community? What can you share with this group about this history that others may not know?

Engaging the Text

Read Genesis 1:24–27

---

[13]https://www.catholiccharitiesusa.org/prayers_reflections/prayer-for-racial-healing/

In v. 26, God says, "Let us make human beings in our image, make them reflecting our nature." What is this image?

How does the image of God reflect the fullness and diversity of race or skin color?

Do you agree that race is a social concept rather than a scientific and biblical one? Why did humans create categories of race?

The Bible has often been used to support racism. What are some ways you have heard or seen this happen?

Closing Prayer

God of Heaven and Earth, you created the human family in your image, and endowed each person with dignity. Grant us your grace in eliminating the blight of racism from our hearts, our communities, and our social, civil, and religious institutions. Fill our hearts with love for you and for our neighbor as we work together with you to heal our land from racial injustice. Amen.

3

Immigration

"You shall also love the stranger, for you were strangers in the land of Egypt."
~ Deuteronomy 10:19

"In everything do to others as you would have them do to you; for this is the law and the prophets.
~ Matthew 7:12

When someone asks you where you're from, how do you typically respond? When you think of home, is there a particular place that comes to mind? Is it a scene in a Norman Rockwell painting, with a fire crackling on the hearth? Is it like that place in Kansas to which Dorothy returns when she clicks her heels together and says, "There's no place like home?" Is it the place of your upbringing—the community, the people, or the geography that shaped you as a child? Is it some place in your distant past where memories were made, a time so long ago and a land so far away that, even if you tried, you could never go back to?

One of the ways you can identify your true home in this world is to pay close attention to the pang you feel when you are far from it. We call that ache "homesickness," or the longing for home. The longing for home is one of the most primal and universal human instincts.

In the epic story, *The Odyssey*, Odysseus desires only one thing: finally to go home. "What I want and all my days I pine for," he says, "is to go back to my house and see my day of homecoming." Home is such a fundamental need for humans that the ancient Greeks came up with a word for the experience of finally finding it: "homecoming." In the Greek, the word is "nostos" (νόστος). Nostos is the root of our English word "nostalgia," which is the longing for home.

When have you felt that longing for home, that homesickness?

It was the summer before my fifth grade year. All spring I had gone door to door selling candy bars to neighbors, raising enough money to go to YMCA camp on Catalina Island off the coast of Southern California. I had been seduced by the photos and testimonials on the color brochure: kayaking, snorkeling, campfires, lanyards. Two weeks of adventure and freedom. I was all in.

On our day of departure, we made the two-hour bus ride from the YMCA to the boat terminal. When we stepped off the buses, every first-year camper went straight to the pay phones to call their mothers collect. All two hundred of us. I didn't even know why I was supposed to call my mother, but I stood in line. That's when I overheard one of the boys on the phone say to his mother, "Come get me. I miss you. I want to come home." I hadn't even missed home yet, hadn't even thought of home, but when I heard that boy pleading with his mom, I was suddenly homesick.

Every mom seemingly said the same thing: "Get on the boat." But by then our excitement had turned to dread, our dread to despair, and when our boat finally docked and we stepped foot on the island, we might as well have been walking on the moon. We had traveled only 16 miles across the Pacific, but it felt as if we were a million miles from home.

Homesickness—the longing for home.

Frederick Buechner points out that the word "longing" comes from the same root as the word "long," in the sense of length and time, as in, "it's a long line," or "it was a long time ago." So, the word "longing" has its origin in time and distance. But the word also comes from the same root as "belong," in the sense of being related to something, as in "the dog belongs to her," or "he belongs to that family." And so, as Buechner suggests, "to long for something" is to yearn for a long time for something that's a long way off and that we cannot live without. To be homesick is to feel both that distance and that absence.

When have you been so far from home, for such a long time, that you felt the ache of homesickness?

A few years ago, *The Washington Post* published a special report on the Syrian refugee crisis, one of the largest forced migrations of people since World War II. The report featured interviews and photographs of widows and orphans, the wealthy, the wounded, children and the elderly, those surviving in camps, and those suffering in urban slums. To capture the full range of refugee life, the journalists witnessed a birth and a wedding, as well as classrooms and operating rooms, and visited a cemetery where families mourned not just for their dead, but for the fact that they are buried on foreign soil.

The reporters took readers to the Beqaa Valley, about five miles from the Syrian border, where an acre of land at the back end of a junkyard was home to 50 Syrian refugees unable to find anywhere else to live. They had slapped together 10 crude tents from scrap wood and plastic under the screaming roar of a crane as it picked up the twisted remains of old cars and refrigerators and smashed them into scrap.

Shards of glass and metal covered the ground. Off in one corner was a hand-dug latrine, an open pit surrounded by a piece of blue plastic that flapped in the wind. At the center of camp was a black hose that rose up from the ground and was connected to a spigot— their only source of water. "We don't know where it comes from," said one man, "but we drink it, we bathe in it, we cook with it."

Everyone at this camp had cuts or scabs on their fingers and toes from walking barefoot. It was winter, but nobody had warm clothes or boots. They were far from home, but even the garbage-strewn dump looked good compared to the war back home that had destroyed their houses and killed their families. "We've all had a shock," said one man. "We don't even feel like we're awake. I ask myself if we're really here."[1]

The root causes of migration are generally understood in terms of "push" and "pull" factors. "Push" factors are those that force individuals to move involuntarily, such as conflict, drought, famine, and religious, political, or ethnic persecution. "Pull" factors are those influences in the destination country that attract individuals to leave their home, such as economic opportunities, employment, love, and the promise of a better life.

"Push" factors play a central role in the current immigration crisis in the U.S. The majority of immigrants to the U.S. today are people who have subjugated one of the deepest of human instincts— nostalgia, the longing for home—in search of safety, security, and opportunities that their real homes can no longer guarantee. Today's immigration crisis is fundamentally distinct from that of previous decades, when the majority of migrants at the U.S. border were men from Mexico, mostly alone, drawn by the prospect of employment in this country, which they tried to enter undetected.

Today, the vast majority of migrants at our borders are women and children fleeing endemic violence in Central America. The personal risks and discomfort incurred by remaining in their country of origin exceeds the risks and discomforts of leaving family, home, country, jobs, language, and possessions; and making the dangerous and often financially costly journey. When they arrive at our borders, the majority do not seek to enter this country undetected. They most often report at border stations to request asylum from the violence and poverty they are seeking to leave behind. This distinction is mostly lost in our national debate over the immigration crisis.

Throughout this book, I am proposing axioms to help us think more reasonably about contentious issues. An axiom is a statement that is taken to be true, to serve as a premise or starting point for further reasoning.

What is *not* an axiom? In the debate over immigration, some on the left might say that those who advocate for strong borders and

---

[1]http://www.washingtonpost.com/sf/syrian-refugees/story/refuge/

stricter border enforcement are racists or nativists. But that is not an axiom; that is simply a cheap caricature. Some on the right might say that those who advocate for sanctuary cities or the humane treatment of border detainees are unpatriotic or Volvo-driving elitists. But that is not an axiom; that's a tired cliché.

As we jump into the contentious and emotional issue of immigration, we begin with what is evident and well established, without controversy or question:

Axiom #1: We are all originally from somewhere else.

Every one of us resides in America because either we migrated here, or our ancestors at some point migrated here. Some might argue that this makes us among the most fortunate and privileged people on the planet. Geography is destiny.

Do you know where your people come from? For about $100 and a swab of saliva you can find out. Millions of Americans are doing this. Why the fascination? We want to know where our story first began, where we come from, to which tribe we belong.

Do you know where your people come from? The U.S. is a melting pot. Most of us self-identify with one of six ancestry groups: German-American (14.7 percent); Black or African-American (12.3 percent); Mexican-American (10.9 percent); Irish-American (10.7 percent); English-American (7.8 percent); or Italian-American (5.5 percent).[2]

If your ancestry doesn't trace back to one of these five ethnicities, it means your people were either a little late to the party, or they came much earlier.

Western Europeans have been here for four hundred years. November 11, 1620, was the date the Mayflower pulled into Plymouth, which was an amazing coincidence when you think about it, because two months earlier they had left a place also called Plymouth. What are the odds of that?

There is not a single person in the U.S. today whose ancestors are not from somewhere else—including the Indigenous Peoples, or

---

[2]https://www.worldatlas.com/articles/largest-ethnic-groups-and-nationalities-in-the-united-states.html

Native Americans, who migrated to North America on foot across the Bering Land Bridge during the Ice Age about 10,000 years ago.

We live in the U.S. only because we migrated here, or because our ancestors migrated here. That awareness is central to the message of Deuteronomy 10: "You shall also love the stranger, for you were strangers in the land of Egypt." Ingrained in the Hebrew consciousness is this constant awareness that they were once aliens in a foreign land. That awareness leads to gratitude and humility, knowing that geography is destiny. We have a future here, thanks in large part to our ancestors.

Once we arrived and settled in this land of opportunity, history reveals that we immediately grew suspicious of the diverse peoples who followed us here. In principle, we aspired to be welcoming. In 1885, the French gave us the Statue of Liberty, the 305-foot-tall icon of freedom and democracy. The U.S. built a pedestal for the statue and mounted inside it a bronze plaque bearing a poem written by Emma Lazarus titled, "The New Colossus." The poem permanently stamped on Lady Liberty the role of unofficial greeter of incoming migrants. Perhaps you recall that most familiar line on that plaque:

> "Give me your entrepreneurs, your innovators,
> your huddled MBAs yearning to breathe free..."

Not exactly.

> "Give me your tired, your poor,
> Your huddled masses yearning to breathe free,
> The wretched refuse of your teeming shore.
> Send these, the homeless, tempest-tost to me,
> I lift my lamp beside the golden door!"

It was a beautiful ideal—an aspiration of the values America sought to stand for. But the ideal was never legislated. It was a poem, not a policy, and as a nation we have wrestled with this in every generation.

This wrestling began in the 1840s with the so-called "Irish Question." The Great Famine (plus the English response to it) put the Irish at the brink of starvation, disease, and death. Two million

Irish immigrants sought refuge in America, arriving in what were called "coffin ships," because so many thousands died on route. Those who survived the journey arrived poor, disease-ridden, and unskilled.

The Irish took the most menial, dangerous, and low-paying jobs: cutting canals, digging trenches, and laying sewer pipes and rail lines. They were despised and marginalized. It didn't help that the majority of them were Catholic, trying to forge a life in a predominantly Protestant, and distinctly anti-Catholic, land. One newspaper in southwestern Missouri, called the *Menace*, ran weekly headlines screaming to readers around the nation about predatory priests, women enslaved in convents, and a dangerous Roman Catholic plot to take over America. Fear and hatred of the Irish led to legislative proposals to deport them. Their churches were regularly burned. Many were refused employment.

In the 1850s, the Chinese arrived on these shores, first to work the gold mines, then to build railroads in the West. Fourteen million Chinese migrated here. As their numbers increased, so did the intensity of anti-Chinese sentiment and the perceived threat that the Chinese brought to the U.S. economy. What became known as "The Yellow Peril" led to the Chinese Exclusion Act of 1882, passed by Congress to limit future immigration of the Chinese.

In the 1920s the "Red Scare" washed upon our shores as Russians fled the Bolshevik Revolution, stoking fears of communism and anarchism. A mounting fear and anxiety that a Bolshevik revolution in America was imminent—a revolution that would fundamentally change the American way of life—stoked this nationwide anti-radical hysteria.

All of this anti-immigrant sentiment led to a regrettable chapter in American history: The Immigration Act of 1924, which limited the number of "undesirables" coming from all over the globe. According to the U.S. Department of State Office of the Historian, the purpose of the act was "to preserve the ideal of U.S. homogeneity." In other words, it was based purely on race, intended to limit the number of non-white immigrants in an effort to preserve the white American gene pool. Congressional opposition to this Act was minimal, and it remained law until The Immigration Act of 1965, which finally removed race as the decisive factor in determining who can immigrate to the U.S. The Immigration Act of 1965 was, as President Johnson said, intended to "correct a cruel and enduring wrong in the conduct of the American nation."

But for a majority of Americans at the time, it likely didn't seem wrong. For most Americans, it probably seemed reasonable, perhaps even necessary—which leads us to our second axiom, one that echoes the words of the late philosopher, George Santayana:

Axiom #2: If we do not learn from our past, we are destined to repeat it.

Proverbs puts it more crudely: "Like a dog that returns to its vomit, so a fool repeats foolish mistakes" (26:11, *CEB*).

Xenophobia is an undeniable part of America's past. It is a powerful force that has led to a lot of unnecessary suffering and hardship and is embedded in much of our current debate over immigration.

Regardless of our political affiliation, the way we talk about immigrants, legal or otherwise, matters deeply. Xenophobic rhetoric only confuses and clouds our common sense and better judgment. When we blame an entire group of people for the wrongs committed by the few who carry out acts of violence, we commit a "cruel and enduring wrong" and repeat the sins of our past.

Jesus never looked upon a person and saw them as an issue. He recognized human dignity even in the eyes of the foreigner and stranger: the Samaritan woman at the well, the Roman soldier at Golgotha, the demoniac from Gerasene, the thief on the cross, and even Pontius Pilate who condemned him to death. "Do unto others," Jesus said, "as you would have them do unto you." There was no "unless" attached to that rule.

Another teacher, "Hillel the Elder," taught in Jerusalem at around the same time Jesus was teaching in Galilee. It is commonly believed that Jesus, as a child, likely heard Hillel teach. Hillel put the Golden Rule another way: "That which is hateful to you, do not do to another; that is the entire Torah, and the rest is interpretation."[3] Perhaps Hillel's advice is a good place to begin when we think about the immigration controversy: to start with knowing at least what is hateful, or cruel, or immoral, and refusing to do it. If it is too difficult to put ourselves in the shoes of the refugee fleeing violence, or those residing in our country illegally, maybe we can at least start by putting ourselves in our own shoes and asking, "What are the core spiritual values that define my character and conduct, that I am unwilling to compromise or sacrifice on the altar of partisan loyalty?"

Senator Ben Sasse of Nebraska describes himself as the second-most conservative senator in Washington. In his recent book, *Them*, he writes about the loneliness epidemic and the role that partisan tribalism plays in social isolation. He says: "ultimately, it's not legislation we're lacking; it's the tight bonds that give our lives meaning, happiness and hope. It's the habits of heart and mind that make us neighbors and friends."[4]

What are the non-negotiable habits of the heart and mind that make us neighbors and allow us to see the stranger not as an other, or an object, or an issue to be solved?

Austrian philosopher Martin Buber (1878–1965) called this the "I-Thou" relationship, and it's central to the Hebrew worldview. When the Hebrews talked about immigrants or aliens, God instructed them to talk about them as human beings, created in God's image.

The Hebrew Bible is very clear in its teachings about the stranger. In the Hebrew, the word is "ger." It means "sojourner, alien, immigrant, foreigner." It appears 92 times in the Torah alone, and appears in Deuteronomy 10:

> "The LORD your God is God of gods and Lord of lords... who executes justice for the orphan and the widow, and who loves the strangers... You shall also love the stranger, for you were strangers in the land of Egypt."

To love the stranger meant first and foremost to do the "ger" no harm, and to protect him from being harmed. Thirty-six times in

[3]https://https.www.sefaria.org/Shabbat.31a.6?lang=bi&with=all&lang2=en
[4]Ben Sasse, *Them* (St. Martin's Press) Kindle Edition, 253.

the Torah we read about protection—not from the stranger but rather for the stranger. This leads us to our third and final axiom:

Axiom #3: God loves the stranger and commands us to do likewise.

I cannot suggest what that should mean for you. One cannot legislate love. I can only remind you that in Scripture it is accepted without controversy or question: God loves the stranger, the "ger," and commands us to do likewise.

Perhaps that invites us to consider three possibilities for a just immigration policy:

- To advocate for border policies that are effective against illegal migration and that allow authorities to carry out the critical task of identifying and preventing terrorists and dangerous criminals from entering the U.S. It is entirely reasonable to advocate for an immigration policy that ensures that our borders are secure.

- To advocate for border policies that ensure the humane and compassionate treatment of the "ger," consistent with American humanitarian values, and recognize that the measure of a society is in how it treats the most vulnerable— especially women and children. This implies a repudiation of unnecessarily harsh or cruel measures of deterrence, including the separation of families and detention measures that led to the dehumanization of detainees. It is entirely reasonable to advocate for an immigration policy that ensures compassionate and humane treatment of all persons.

- To advocate for policies that create opportunities for hard-working, undocumented immigrants who are contributing to our country to come out of the shadows, regularize their status upon satisfaction of reasonable criteria and, over time, pursue options to become legal residents or citizens. The majority of Americans today support a path to residency or citizenship for law-abiding undocumented immigrants.

What I am proposing is, in the words of Shakespeare, justice seasoned with mercy. And it is based on three simple axioms:

1) We are all originally from somewhere else—we were once the "ger"; 2) If we do not learn from our past we are destined to repeat it, and so we start with acknowledging what is hateful, cruel, or immoral, and refusing to do it; and 3) God loves the stranger and commands us to do likewise.

Justice seasoned with mercy.

If we do not agree on everything, perhaps we can all agree on two things: Justice seasoned with mercy has always been our ideal as Americans, and it will always be our obligation as Christians.

Further Study and Reflection for Groups or Individuals

A Prayer for Guidance and Grace

Guide us, O Lord, in our thoughts and words. We gather as followers of the refugee Christ, who from his birth to his death had no place to lay his head. We gather as followers of the Christ who comes to us as a stranger, seeking to understand and to respond to the migrants, immigrants, refugees, and asylum seekers in our land. We gather in a spirit of gratitude for the daily gifts of food, security, and the simple comforts of home. Amen.

Icebreaker

What brought you or your ancestors to the U.S.? What was your/ their country of origin? When did you/they arrive, and where did you/they settle?

When you think of "home," what particular place, image, or feeling comes to mind?

Have you had a personal experience with immigrants that has influenced your thinking, positively or negatively, about the issue of immigration? If so, are you willing to share it with the group?

Why do you think immigration can be such a divisive or contentious issue for Americans?

Deep Dive

What did you learn in this chapter about the history of immigration in the U.S.?

What aspects of the history of immigration policy in the U.S. reflect elements of xenophobia (fear of the stranger)? How might the lessons of the past inform our current national debate on the issue of immigration?

The root causes of migration are generally understood in terms of "push" factors and "pull" factors. "Push" factors are those that force individuals to move involuntarily, such as conflict, drought, famine, and religious, political, or ethnic persecution. "Pull" factors are those influences in the destination country that attract individuals to leave their home, such as economic opportunities, employment, love, and the promise of a better life. Which of these two factors seems to play a greater role in the current immigration crisis in the U.S.? Should immigrants who are forced to leave their country of origin due to "push" factors be treated differently?

Engaging the Text

Read Deuteronomy 10:14–20.

What does it mean to "circumcise the foreskin of your heart" (v. 16)?

What does it look like, in practical terms, to "execute justice" for the most vulnerable in our land (v. 18)?

Why does God command us to "love the stranger" (v. 19)?

In what ways is it possible for an immigration policy in the U.S. to be both just and merciful?

Closing Prayer

God of justice and mercy, we who were once foreigners and sojourners in a strange land, remember those who have left their homes in search of security and opportunity. Give them strength and courage on their journey. Give us wisdom and grace to respond in ways that are just and merciful — that all your children will be home at last and find refuge in your love. Amen.

4

Healthcare

"...and when he saw him, he was moved with pity."

~ Luke 10:33

The issue of healthcare in America has, for the last decade, been front and center for most Americans. According to Gallup, it was the number one issue for voters in the 2018 midterms. Eighty percent of Americans said that it was "extremely/very important."[1]

Healthcare is so important because it affects all of us directly. When we are healthy, we worry that we may be paying too much for coverage we may never need. When we are sick, we worry that we may not have enough coverage when we need it most. When we are younger, we wonder why we need it all. When we are older, we wonder how we could ever live without it.

Healthcare is a consequential issue for all of us—especially for those who do not have it because they cannot afford it. I recall a member of my former congregation whose life was saved by the extraordinary technologies of healthcare, but whose personal

---

[1]https://news.gallup.com/poll/244367/top-issues-voters-healthcare-economy-immigration.aspx

finances were shattered as a result of not having insurance when he needed it most. In 2006, he was a small business owner and in relatively good health for a 60-year-old man. Struggling to make ends meet, he chose to forgo purchasing health insurance in order to keep his shop open—only to suffer a major heart attack months later. The costs of several weeks of hospitalization and four new heart valves totaled $240,000. To pay his medical bills, he leveraged the equity in his home and refinanced his mortgage with a subprime loan—just months before the 2008 economic recession. His life was saved at the cost of his home, his business, and his peace of mind. The lack of affordable health insurance turned out to be an altogether different kind of death sentence.

When we talk about healthcare in America, we are not simply talking about some neutral issue. We are talking about real people and what kind of present and future they will have, and this makes affordable healthcare a deeply moral issue for all Americans.

This is not a new problem. America's healthcare debate began in the late 19th century, during the Industrial Revolution, when mill jobs led to workplace injuries and labor unions began advocating for sickness and injury protections.

By 1929, a unique product was introduced: individual prepayment for hospital care, offered originally for teachers by a company called Blue Cross. Another company, Blue Shield, offered a similar program to lumber and mining workers for reimbursable physician's services. Employees paid monthly fees to groups of physicians for guaranteed healthcare.

By the 1940s, about 9 percent of the American population had health insurance.[2] But following World War II, a unique situation emerged. Veterans returning from war flooded the labor markets. As a means to control inflation and limit wage increases, Congress passed the Stabilization Act of 1942, prohibiting U.S. businesses from offering higher salaries to compete for labor. As a result, companies began looking for more creative ways to recruit employees and incentivize existing employees to stay. The solution was the foundation of employer-sponsored health insurance as we

---

[2]https://www.nytimes.com/2017/09/05/upshot/the-real-reason-the-us-has-employer-sponsored-health-insurance.html

know it today. Employees enjoyed this fringe benefit because they did not have to pay taxes on this form of compensation, and they were able to insure their families.

By 1950, more than 50 percent of Americans had some form of health coverage through their employers. By 1960, more than two-thirds did.[3] But vulnerable groups of people were left out: retirees, the unemployed, the disabled, and those whose employers could not afford to offer coverage.

Two programs were signed into law by President Johnson to address this disparity: the Medicare program, providing medical insurance for people age 65 and older; and Medicaid, offering health coverage to low-income people. Today, these programs cover approximately 118 million Americans.[4]

In 1970, national health expenditures accounted for 6.9 percent of GDP. Today, it's 17.9 percent.[5] What is responsible for that growth? Advances in medical technologies, increasing provider costs, life-saving prescriptions, and an increasingly older and unhealthy American population are factors. Today, the sickest 5 percent of Americans consume 50 percent of the nation's total healthcare costs. The healthiest 50 percent consume 3 percent of the nation's healthcare costs.[6] The U.S. medical profession does a heroic job of saving and prolonging lives, but it comes at a cost. Medicare spending for patients in the last year of life is six times greater than the average.[7] The cost of care for this patient group accounts for one-fourth of the entire Medicare budget.[8]

[3]Ibid.

[4]https://www.cnsnews.com/news/article/terence-p-jeffrey/census-bureau-118395000-government-health-insurance-2015-28966000

[5]https://www.healthsystemtracker.org/chart-collection/u-s-spending-healthcare-changed-time/#item-nhe-trends_total-national-health-expenditures-us-billions-1970-2018

[6]https://www.healthsystemtracker.org/chart-collection/health-expenditures-vary-across-population/#item-discussion-of-health-spending-often-focus-on-averages-but-a-small-share-of-the-population-incurs-most-of-the-cost_2016

[7]https://www.cms.gov/Research-Statistics-Data-and-Systems/Research/ActuarialStudies/downloads/Last_Year_of_Life.pdf

[8]https://www.aarp.org/health/medicare-insurance/info-2018/medicare-spending-on-dying-patients.html

By 2007, a record 47 million Americans were uninsured—either because they or their employers could no longer afford coverage, because they were not poor enough or old enough to qualify for Medicaid or Medicare, or because they had a preexisting condition.[9] This led to the Affordable Care Act (ACA) of 2010 which, as you may have heard, is not without its critics. Nevertheless, 52 percent of Americans today have a favorable view of the ACA,[10] and while some advocate for "repeal and replace," and others for "retain and repair," the ACA has accomplished some important measures, including:

- the removal of lifetime limits on benefits

- free screening and preventative services, including maternity and newborn care

- guaranteed coverage for preexisting conditions

- the ability for students to remain on a parent's health insurance plan through age 26

Whether you're a Democrat or a Republican or something else, finding solutions to our healthcare insurance crisis is a Christian issue.

Throughout this book, I am using axioms to find common ground for more generous conversations that contribute to the common good. An axiom is a statement that is taken to be true and self-evident, regardless of ideology or theology.

So, we begin with our first axiom, gleaned from the writings of the second-century theologian, St. Irenaeus:

Axiom # 1: "The glory of God is a human being fully alive."

One common misconception about Jesus is that his earthly ministry was defined primarily by his teaching and preaching. But read the gospels carefully and you will find that the majority of

---

[9]http://archive.boston.com/news/nation/articles/2007/08/29/47_million_americans_are_uninsured/

[10]https://www.kff.org/health-reform/poll-finding/6-charts-about-public-opinion-on-the-affordable-care-act/

his time and energy were committed to healing and caring for the sick. There are 37 miracles of Jesus recorded in the gospels, 31 of which are healing miracles, and two of which are mass healings. Jesus healed lepers, demoniacs, paralytics, the blind, the deaf, the hemorrhaging, and the dead.

Jesus was a healer. He came to be known as "The Great Physician" because he cared as much about the health of the human body as he did about the condition of the human soul. He would have rejected the dualism of so many Christians today who believe that the soul is more important than the body. Jesus was "the Word made flesh," the physical embodiment of God. The mystery of the incarnation meant that the divine body and soul were inseparable, and this is how Jesus understood the human body and soul. He saw in the faces of the sick not simply an illness to be cured, but a person to be restored to life and to his or her community. Over and over again, he followed a healing with the command, "Go back..." to your people, to your village, to the temple, to your home—because he knew that when one person was made well, the entire community was made well.

What do you call a community that is "well?" Jesus called it the "Βασιλεία τοῦ Θεοῦ," "the Kingdom of God." He did not understand this kingdom to mean some heavenly place where we experience eternal life in the spirit. He meant something like a neighborhood in which all the neighbors are fully alive, because those who live there are fiercely committed to the wellness of all their neighbors.

"But who is my neighbor?" asked the inquiring man. Jesus told him a story about a man who, on this perilous journey we call life, fell among terrible forces that overtook him. In the story, Jesus called them bandits; but he could have called them cancer, or depression, or dementia, or diabetes. Whatever you call it, the man was left for dead, neglected by the neighbors who should have cared but did not. But a complete stranger chose to care. He bound the dying man's wounds, and essentially carried him to an ER, and offered to pay the bill until the man was fully alive again.

"Who is the neighbor in the story?" asked Jesus.

"The one who showed compassion," replied the man.

"Go and do likewise," said Jesus.

The glory of God is a human being fully alive, and the Kingdom of God is the neighborhood that makes the fullness of life possible for all who live there.

But our capacity to help others flourish is determined by the breadth and depth of our compassion, which leads to our second axiom:

Axiom #2: "Good health is a crown on the head of a well person that only a sick person can see,"[11] and illness is a cross borne by the unsuspecting.

Rarely do we acknowledge the undeserved blessing of good health. Rarely do we anticipate illness when it falls on us. Rarely do we pause to consider what it is like for those who fall ill. Health is a privilege that goes unnoticed until it is lost to us.

To grow old is a gift. To grow old means that we have somehow, so far, avoided the cruel bandits on the road to Jericho. Some people do not get this far. My own father, at age 48, was overcome by those bandits. One day he wore the crown of health and the next, he bore the cross of terminal illness.

Whenever Jesus looked upon someone bearing that cross, the gospels describe his response with the word "splagchnizomai" (Σπλαγχνίζομαι). It means "compassion." But the verb form comes from the noun "splanxna," meaning bowels, or gut. In the ancient world, it was the gut, not the heart, that was perceived as the center of human emotion. To have compassion, ("splagchnizomai") is to feel something so deep in your gut that you are moved to action.

In her early 30s, Kate Bowler was a wife, a new mother, and a professor at Duke Divinity School. Then she was diagnosed with stage four colon cancer and given only months to live. Experimental immunotherapy has kept her alive. In her book, *Everything Happens for a Reason,* she says,

---

[11]https://twitter.com/RobinSharma/status/648520369788350464

I don't know how to explain it... It's like we're all floating on the ocean, holding on to our own inner tubes. We're all floating around, but people don't seem to know that we're all sinking. Some are sinking faster than others, but we're all sinking..." I keep having the same unkind thought—I am preparing for death and everyone else is on Instagram. I know... that life is hard for everyone... but I sometimes feel like I'm the only one in the world who is dying.[12]

When the cost of her therapy reached several hundred thousand dollars, her community of friends and advocates stepped in to help — *Splagchnizomai*. Like that Samaritan neighbor, they were moved by compassion to keep her alive.

But there are 28 million uninsured American citizens, and an estimated 14 million immigrants in the U.S. who are not as fortunate, and we might ask whether our failure to create a program to insure all Americans is due to a lack of imagination, a lack of compassion, or a combination of both. "It's like we're all floating on the ocean, holding on to our own inner tubes," says Bowler. Under our current system, there seem to be only so many inner tubes to go around—and that's a moral issue. This leads to our third axiom, gleaned from the teachings of the Apostle Paul.

Axiom #3: "Your body is a temple where the Holy Spirit lives."

Paul didn't mean that our body is simply a container for more important, spiritual things. He understood the body as a temple, a sanctuary, by which he meant that our actual flesh and blood is made holy, or consecrated, by the spirit that dwells within it.

Your body matters to God. It's an essential part of the sacred image of the Divine. And because you are responsible for your body, that makes you a co-creator with God. So, love your own embodiment. Be kind to your body. Care for it.

We know that a major contributor to healthcare costs in America is the increasing unhealthiness of the American populace. We are

---

[12]Kate Bowler, *Everything Happens for a Reason: And Other Lies I've Loved* (New York: Random House Publishing Group) Kindle Edition, 64–65.

less fit, less active, and more sedentary than those of previous generations. Chronic diseases, such as heart disease and cancer, are among the most common, costly, and preventable of all health problems in the United States. Each year, chronic diseases cause 7 of 10 deaths among Americans.[13] Four personal behaviors that can affect chronic diseases are: lack of physical activity, poor nutrition, tobacco use, and excessive alcohol consumption.

We have a role in our own wellness, and we owe it to our community to invest in our wellness.

Any viable healthcare policy must move to a new paradigm focused on creating healthier life years. Today's healthcare industry is based on a sick care model, rather than an incentivized model that rewards personal responsibility.

We need to change the way we think about our choices when it comes to our own health. We need to ask ourselves some very basic questions, such as: What is my responsibility for eating healthy foods, managing stress, getting enough sleep, and exercising every day to live a healthier life?

We need also to think about the neighborhoods where that freedom of choice and responsibility is limited by poverty and inequality. Fast food chains and convenience stores are a blight on our urban centers, where fresh produce, recreation centers, and access to clinics are scarce. The body is the temple, but there are millions of Americans whose very temples are imperiled by social inequities that are systemic and chronic. This leads to our fourth and final axiom.

Axiom #4: The price of democracy is our mutual commitment to our common life.

As political theorist and community activist Saul Alinsky once said, "People cannot be truly free unless they are willing to sacrifice some of their interests to guarantee the freedom of others."[14]

---

[13]https://ephtracking.cdc.gov/showLifestyleRiskFactorsMain
[14]https://voxpopulisphere.com/2017/02/25/saul-alinsky-rules-for-radicals/

This is the very spirit of democracy. It is what sends women and men willingly into the battlefield to defend our country, or into burning towers to rescue lives, or into the line of fire to protect our cities and neighborhoods. It's what sends some into school classrooms instead of corporate boardrooms, willing to be paid less to serve their communities. It's what compels us to contribute to victims of disasters, and inspires us to feed the hungry in our local communities. It's a willingness and an eagerness to sacrifice our personal interests for the freedom and flourishing of others.

Healthcare is not a constitutional right, but it is a human right implied in the unalienable rights of "life, liberty, and the pursuit of happiness." It is not a universal law, but it is our shared commitment to the common good, which has always been the American ideal.

Our healthcare system is not so broken that, to enable 28 million more people to gain access to quality, affordable care we have to throw out what is working for the 300 million people who have it. There will always be portions of the patient population who need the government to be the payer, but not necessarily the provider. Existing programs should be expanded to include all those currently left out, with some form of a sliding scale of personal financial responsibility for their care.

The question the parable of the Good Samaritan leaves us with is this: "What kind of neighborhood do we want to live in?" The book of Deuteronomy gives us a blueprint:

> If among you, one of your brothers should become poor, in any of your towns within your land... you shall not harden your heart or shut your hand against your poor brother, but you shall open your hand to him and lend him sufficient for his need, whatever it may be... For there will never cease to be poor in the land. Therefore I command you, "open wide your hand to your brother, to the needy and to the poor, in your land."(Deut. 15:7–11)

How do we create this kind of neighborhood? We become better neighbors, recognizing what is true and evident:

- The glory of God is a human being fully alive. This calls us to take delight in the health and flourishing of all our neighbors.

- Health is a crown worn by the unaware, and illness is a cross borne by the unsuspecting. This calls us into deeper kinship with all of our neighbors, and especially with those who suffer.

- Our body is a temple where the Holy Spirit lives. This calls us to claim personal responsibility for our health and wellbeing.

- The price of democracy is our shared commitment to the common good. This calls us to a life rooted in kenosis, or self-giving, for the sake of others, especially the most vulnerable.

Does that not describe the kind of neighborhood you'd like to live in?

Further Study and Reflection for Groups or Individuals

A Prayer for Guidance and Grace

Jesus the Christ, Divine Physician and Healer of the sick, we gather in gratitude for life and health, for kinship and community that makes us well. We place our sick under your care and humbly ask that you restore them to health again. Above all, grant us the grace to feel empathy and compassion for all who suffer, and to respond with mercy and kindness. Amen.

Icebreaker

When was the last time you experienced an illness that required you to see a physician? Were it not for proper medical treatment, would your illness have progressed?

Do you know, or have you known, someone who has suffered a major illness without adequate healthcare coverage? What was the outcome?

Do you believe that health insurance companies should be required to provide affordable healthcare coverage to people with preexisting conditions? Why or why not?

Do you believe that the federal government should guarantee access to affordable healthcare for all Americans? Why or why not?

Deep Dive

What did you learn in this chapter about the history of healthcare coverage in the U.S.?

Today, the sickest 5 percent of Americans consume 50 percent of the nation's total healthcare costs. The healthiest 50 percent consume 3 percent of the nation's healthcare costs. What does this say about the paradigm of our current healthcare system? How might the system be redesigned to promote greater personal accountability and prevention?

Why do people living in urban centers in the U.S. face greater challenges in maintaining personal health and accessing adequate healthcare?

What do you think of Saul Alinsky's assertion that, "People cannot be truly free unless they are willing to sacrifice some of their interests to guarantee the freedom of others"? What personal sacrifices are you willing to make to ensure that others are adequately insured?

Engaging the Text

Read Luke 10:30–37.

Why do you think the priest and the Levite walked away from the injured man?

What is a Samaritan? Why did the Samaritan stop to assist the injured man? What personal qualities or characteristics factor into his response?

Why was it so extraordinary for the Samaritan to stop and tend to the man's wounds?

How can we express more compassion and care for one another? What does this require in terms of both personal attitudes and collective resources?

Is our healthcare system so broken that, to enable 28 million more people gaining access to quality, affordable care we have to throw out what is working for the 300 million people who have it? How might we solve the situation for the 28 million Americans who currently do not have quality, affordable care?

Closing Prayer
Lord, open our eyes,
> that we may see you in our brothers and sisters.

Lord, open our ears,
> that we may hear the cries of the hungry,
> the cold, the frightened, the oppressed.

Lord, open our hearts,
> that we may love each other as you love us.

Renew in us your spirit.
Lord, free us and make us one. Amen.
> ~ Mother Teresa

5

Medical Aid in Dying ·

"So Saul took his own sword and fell upon it."

~ 1 Samuel 31:4

"For I am convinced that neither death, nor life, nor angels, nor rulers, nor things present, nor things to come, nor powers, nor height, nor depth, nor anything else in all creation, will be able to separate us from the love of God in Christ Jesus our Lord."
~ Romans 8:38–39

"Then Jesus gave a loud cry and breathed his last."
~ Mark 15:37

Many Christians try at all costs to avoid mixing politics and church. The popular sociologist and pastor, Tony Campolo, once said that mixing church and politics is like mixing ice cream and manure. It doesn't do much for the manure, but it sure does ruin the ice cream.

But what if, when Christians are in church, they should actually be at their *most* political. By political I do not mean partisan. The word "politics" comes from the Greek, "polis," meaning "affairs of the cities." Many assume that "politics" comes from the two words, "poly," meaning "many," and "ticks," as in "bloodsucking parasites." To "do politics" is to be concerned about the affairs of the communities in which we live, and to do politics in church is to ask, What does the gospel of Jesus Christ say about how I should live in my community, and what should my responsibility be to the members of that community?

This is a politics of compassion, and it is vastly different from what typically passes for politics in America today. It transcends "issue politics" and calls us to consider what kind of community we want to live in, and what kind of neighbors we want to be. We cannot answer those questions by simply pulling the lever in the polling booth because, when all is said and done, Jesus will not ask us how we voted. Jesus will ask us, "When I was hungry, thirsty, sick and in prison, did you care for me? When I was your neighbor in disguise, did you love me?" A politics of compassion is the only kind of politics that matters to Jesus.

In this chapter we are addressing an issue that is far less politically divisive for most Americans, but one that presents for many of us a moral and theological dilemma: medical aid in dying. In 2016, in my home state of Colorado, voters passed Proposition 106, the End of Life Options Act, by a margin of nearly 2:1. The law authorizes medical aid in dying and allows a terminally ill adult to end his or her life in a peaceful manner.

This is a tender conversation, because we're not simply talking about an issue. We are talking about real people—those we know or have known, those we love or have loved, even ourselves. We are talking about death, which will touch all of us; and illness, which will touch most of us; and suffering, which all of us fear; and a choice, which is purely hypothetical until it becomes profoundly personal.

Historically, ethicists and theologians have framed this conversation within the category of "euthanasia," which comes from two Greek words: "eu," meaning "good;" and "thanatos, meaning "death." Euthanasia literally means "good death."

Euthanasia describes a host of different concepts and practices, but I want to focus exclusively on its most common application today, often referred to as "medical aid in dying," "physician-assisted death," or "death with dignity." These terms generally refer to a practice in which a physician provides a terminally ill adult patient with a prescription for a lethal dose of medication, upon the patient's request, which the patient intends to use to end his or her life. The patient must be mentally competent and have a prognosis of less than six months to live and no reasonable expectation for improvement.

The debate about medical aid in dying dates back to ancient Greece, when patients suffering extreme pain from an incurable terminal illness sought out physicians willing to give them a poisoned drink. It was Pythagoras who first opposed this practice, arguing that because the gods have placed humans as the protector of the earthly life, humans are therefore not permitted to escape their purpose or fate.

In the fourth century B.C., the first official objection to euthanasia made its way into the Hippocratic Oath, which says, "I will not administer poison to anyone when asked to do so, nor suggest such a course."

By the Middle Ages (the fifth to the fourteenth centuries), Christian teaching opposed euthanasia, maintaining that human beings, created by God, belong to God and not to themselves. God is the sole power who creates life, and the only power who may take life away.

In the 17th century, the English philosopher, Francis Bacon, was the first to discuss an alternative to euthanasia: what we now call "palliative care," or easing the suffering of the dying. Bacon encouraged doctors to "acquire the skill and bestow the attention whereby the dying may pass more easily and quietly out of life."

After World War II, the atrocities of the Nazis profoundly influenced public perception of euthanasia. In 1920, two German professors had published a booklet entitled, "Permitting the Destruction of Life Unworthy of Life," advocating the killing of people whose lives were "devoid of value." This became the ideological basis for eugenics by means of involuntary euthanasia of the sick and disabled in the Third Reich, and it gave rise to the "slippery slope" argument that says, "If voluntary euthanasia is permitted, then involuntary euthanasia will eventually happen too."

Fast forward to June 1990, when Dr. Jack Kevorkian became a household name by participating in his first of 130 physician-assisted suicides in the U.S. Four years later Oregon passed the Death With Dignity Act—the first law in American history permitting physician-assisted death. Today, six states and Washington, D.C.. have similar laws.

In my denomination, The United Methodist Church, the *Social Principles* oppose physician-assisted death and euthanasia, stating:

> If death is deliberately sought as the means to relieve suffering, that must be understood as direct and intentional taking of life … The United Methodist tradition opposes the taking of life as an offense against God's sole dominion over life, and an abandonment of hope and humility before God.[1]

The consensus among other mainline Protestant denominations emphasizes that a truly compassionate response to the needs of the terminally ill is one that invests in and advocates for quality palliative care rather than lethal prescriptions.

As a pastor, I affirm this theological position, even as I support legal protections for physicians who assist their patients with dying. I have been with countless people in their final moments, including my own father. I have witnessed the peace of a good death, fostered by the care and compassion of people who surround the dying. I advocate for that ideal, even as I recognize that not everyone has access to that kind of community of love and care. But while I affirm the legal right to medical aid in dying, the question that concerns me is the same question we have asked throughout this book: What kind of neighbor does Jesus call me to be for those who suffer?

---

[1]http://www.umc.org/what-we-believe/what-is-the-united-methodist-stance-on-assisted-suicide

We have been using axioms throughout this book to find common ground on sensitive issues. An axiom is a simple statement taken to be true and self-evident: an object at rest will stay at rest unless acted upon by an outside force; Earth is the third rock from the sun; cats are at the center of their universe.

So let's begin with our first axiom:

Axiom #1: Mortality has always been, and will always be, a preexisting human condition.

The last time I checked, the human mortality rate was still hovering right around 100 percent.

Prior to the scientific revolution of the 16 century, it had long been believed that God defined the length of a life. The majority of people died from accidents or infectious disease. But people generally believed that how long we lived and how we died were predetermined by God. As scientists began to understand human biology, these beliefs changed. Deaths from infectious diseases, accidents, and certain behaviors came to be seen as mostly preventable, not divinely preordained. Suddenly, we came to believe that we were responsible for our own lives and deaths. We were no longer up against the inevitability of some preordained divine plan. This meant that maybe we could put off death. We could avoid it—not permanently, of course, but for as long as possible. Death became something to outrun, which made it something to be feared more than anything.

Our fear of death begins in early childhood, perhaps because of how adults talk about it in hushed whispers, with tears and secrecy. As teenagers, we become more acutely aware of death, but we do not think of it as relating specifically to us—as though it will actually happen to us someday. It's only as we mature into adulthood that our own death begins to seem not only possible but inevitable. The knowledge that our physical body will cease to exist someday, that this life of ours will eventually end, stirs up all kinds of fears: How will it happen? Will it happen slowly or suddenly? Will it be peaceful or painful? Will I be alone? Will anyone miss me? What will become of me afterward?

Any conversation about physician-assisted death must begin by acknowledging that we live in a culture that fears death. It is the greatest of human fears. We avoid even saying the word "death," opting instead for popular clichés like "passing on" or "going to a better place." Some even prefer more colorful euphemisms: pushing up daisies, buying the farm, cashing in your chips, taking the cab, going off the grid, heading for the happy hunting ground, blinking for an exceptionally long time.

It helps to laugh at, or at least name, our greatest fear. Epicurus called the fear of death the fundamental source of human anguish. Virginia Morris, in her book *Talking About Death Won't Kill You*, recommends that we brace ourselves for it. Name your fears, she says, no matter how irrational. Rehearse the crisis like a soldier who acts out what to do, so that nothing is a complete surprise. "We all know... we are headed for a crash," she writes. "We have to accept that the crash will happen."[2] So, imagine it in all its permutations. Doing so may empower you to claim greater agency in preparing for your death by addressing the very practical matters and concerns of your life that your survivors will someday have to deal with, such as the location of the will, birth certificate, marriage and divorce certificates, Social Security information, life-insurance policies, financial documents, passwords, and keys to a safe deposit box or home safe.

How does one prepare for the "crash?" *New York Times* columnist Arthur Brooks took a trip to Thailand, where he was surprised to learn that Buddhist monks often contemplate the photos of corpses. It's called "corpse meditation," and it is intended as a key to better living. It makes the monks aware of the transitory nature of their physical lives and stimulates a realignment between momentary desires and existential goals. It makes one ask, "Am I making the right use of my scarce and precious life?"[3]

---

[2]Virginia Morris, Talking about Death Won't Kill You (New York: Workman, 2001), quoted in Sallie Tisdale, *Advice for Future Corpses (and Those Who Love Them): A Practical Perspective on Death and Dying* (New York: Gallery Books, 2018), Kindle Edition, 34.

[3]https://www.nytimes.com/2016/01/10/opinion/sunday/to-be-happier-start-thinking-more-about-your-death.html

If corpse meditation is a bit too much for you, you might try some alternatives. If you're planning a vacation, consider where you would like to go if this were your last trip. With whom would you spend time? If you had less than a year to live, would you spend another precious moment mindlessly checking your Facebook account, or would you do something more creative or generous instead?

Well before the era of airplanes, immunizations, and social media, the prophet Isaiah put it this way:

> Why do you spend your money for that which is not bread, and your labor for that which does not satisfy? ...eat what is good, and delight yourselves in rich food (55:2, *NRSV*).

A good life is the best preparation for a good death, which leads us to our second axiom:

Axiom #2: A good death is a death claimed and unhidden.

If we can accept our fear of death, we can better plan for it before it happens. We can write a will, suggest what music might be played at our funeral, who may want to speak at the service, what will happen with our body. We can write an advance directive so that our loved ones know our wishes if we are unable to communicate them. We can make amends, reconcile, or forgive. To claim your death is to affirm that your death belongs only to you, and that there are some things about your death that you get to decide. Sallie Tisdale, in her *Advice for Future Corpses*, asks, "Can our death reflect the way we have tried to live? Rather than glibly wishing for a 'good death,' perhaps we are better off thinking of a 'fitting death.'"[4] For some, a fitting death might mean being surrounded by family and friends; for others, it might mean intentional solitude, or meeting with a pastor, or communing with nature.

We can control some aspects of our dying, but not everything. Even if we choose assistance in dying and take the lethal medication by

---

[4]Tisdale, *Advice for Future Corpses,* 49.

our own power, the illusion is that we are in control of our death—especially the preservation of our dignity.

Loss of dignity is perhaps one of the most common reasons people give for supporting assisted death measures. We often refer to assisted death by the more acceptable phrase, "death with dignity." We assume that means we can avoid all of those painful and undignified experiences that come from being dependent on others in the later stages of our dying: bedpans, sponge baths, mouth swabs, incontinence, delirium. We assume that "dignity" means that our suffering, bodily deterioration, weakness, nausea, and body fluids must remain behind doors, hidden from the sight of others. "I don't want you to see me like this," we might say. Such things feel below our dignity somehow, as if they make us less human.

King Saul could not bear the thought of what the Philistines would do to him and the disgrace his publicly shameful death would bring upon his legacy and his people. So he fell on his own sword to avoid the indignities he felt were beneath him.

There is nothing wrong with such feelings. We are a culture enamored with beauty, autonomy, privacy, and stoicism. We want death to look clean and orderly. But death is often messy. Terminal illness is a visible condition in which personal privacy is often forfeited.

One of the treasures of the Christian tradition is the enduring symbol of the cross. I grew up in the Catholic Church, where the likeness of a dying human body was affixed to that cross. It was a messy, traumatic death: blood, fluids, anguish, and lament. So why is it such a powerful symbol? Because, from the cross, Jesus says, "Look at me. Look at this. This will happen to you, too. Death comes to everyone. This is what it means to be human. Do not turn away from what is real."

The dignity of Jesus was not lost in the unloveliness of his dying on the cross. His dignity was preserved by giving us a generous and honest glimpse of our own lives and our own deaths. Dignity is the courage to be unashamed by what happens to the human body. For Jesus, dignity was the willingness to be seen exactly as he was, even in the moment of his death.

Having control of our death is an illusion, and losing our dignity in dying is a myth. This leads us to our final axiom:

Axiom #3: A good death is determined by the meaning we assign to it.

Illness is replete with meaning. Death has meaning. It is different for everyone, and I have learned as a pastor never to impose meaning on anyone's illness, or to deny anyone the meaning they've assigned to it. I have known some people who see illness as a punishment, others as a test of their faith, and still others who view it as part of God's plan. Illness and dying always have meaning—sometimes unambiguous, sometimes incidental, and often times invisible to everyone else.

I remember a woman in the first church where I served as a pastor. When she became too sick to attend worship, I began visiting her in her home. She had suffered a stroke, and the paralysis on her left side robbed her of mobility and speech. She communicated with me through written messages on a small green notepad in the handwriting of her old age. Near the end of her life, unable to eat, she made the conscious decision to forego surgery to place a feeding tube that would have prolonged her life. We talked about that decision, but only briefly. She wanted instead to talk about how God had been so good to her, even in this season of suffering.

On her notepad, she wrote the following words that I have not since forgotten: "Can't walk. Can't eat. Can't talk." She showed me the words. I nodded in agreement. Then she wrote the most curious words of all: "God is blessing me." I paused to reflect on that progression of thought. "Can't walk, can't eat, can't talk. God is blessing me."

Illness is replete with meaning.

The Apostle Paul says: "I am convinced that neither death, nor life, nor angels, nor rulers, nor things present, nor things to come, nor powers, nor height, nor depth, nor anything else in all creation, will be able to separate us from the love of God in Christ Jesus" (Romans 8:38–39).

Nothing in life or in death can separate us from the love of God: not death by lethal medication, or death made more peaceful and bearable by palliative care. Not a death absent of suffering, or a death imbued or seemingly diminished by suffering. Nothing can separate us from God's love. But I have witnessed the redemptive power of illness to draw people closer to God, and to knit the bonds of kinship between family and friends ever tighter. In witnessing the illness of others, I have found delight in the living soul of a person even as the body deteriorates, and I have been inspired and emboldened to live a life rooted in kenosis, which calls me to give myself even more to nurturing that love in my life, in my community, and in the world.

However we choose to walk that final leg of our journey, with or without the help of lethal intervention, God's grace is near. So, we remember this:

> Mortality is a preexisting human condition.
> A good death is a death claimed, and a death unhidden.
> Illness is replete with meaning.

Further Study and Reflection for Groups or Individuals

A Prayer for Guidance and Grace

> O God, who gave us birth,
> you are ever more ready to hear
> than we are to pray.
> You know our needs before we ask,
> and our ignorance in asking.
> Give to us now your grace,
> that as we shrink before the mystery of death,
> we may see the light of eternity.
> Speak to us once more
> your solemn message of life and of death.

Help us to live as those who are prepared to die.
And when our days here are accomplished,
enable us to die as those who go forth to live,
so that living or dying, our life may be in you,
and that nothing in life or in death will be able to
separate us
from your great love in Christ Jesus our Lord. Amen.[5]

Icebreaker

How much thought or action have you given to your own wishes
for end-of-life medical treatment?

Have you completed instructions (such as a living will or an
advance directive) about what actions should be taken for
your health if you are no longer able to make decisions for
yourself because of illness or incapacity?

What would you do if had only one year to live? (How) would
you reorder your priorities? Would you take a trip? Would you
reconcile with someone?

Who was the first member of your family or circle of friends to
die? Were you present?

Why is medical aid in dying such a controversial issue for many
Americans?

Deep Dive

What did you learn in this chapter about the history of medical
aid in dying?

Since the Middle Ages, Christian teaching has opposed euthanasia,
maintaining that human beings are created by God and belong
to God, and that only God has the power to take life away.

Do you think Christians' attitudes on this issue have changed over
time? If so, why?

---

[5]https://www.umcdiscipleship.org/book-of-worship/a-service-of-death-and-resurrection

How have the views of Americans changed on this issue over the last few decades? Do you think more states in the U.S. will adopt measures that support medical aid in dying?

"Having control of our death is an illusion, and losing our dignity in dying is a myth." Do you agree with this statement? Is fear of losing of one's dignity a driving factor in support for medical aid in dying?

Do you agree that "A good death is determined by the meaning we assign to it?" How can death have meaning?

Engaging the Text

Read Mark 15:22–24, 34–35, 37, 39.

What does Jesus' very public death teach about what it means to be human?

What is the meaning of Jesus' death to you?

Was Jesus' death dignified or undignified?

"Dignity is the courage to not be ashamed by what happens to the body. For Jesus, dignity was the willingness to be seen exactly as he was." Why do you think many people are ashamed to be seen in their final days? What does this shame say about our culture? About our communities?

What can we learn about ourselves by being present with those who are dying?

Closing Prayer

God, grant me the serenity to accept the things I cannot change,
the courage to change the things I can,
and the wisdom to know the difference. Amen.
~ Reinhold Niebuhr (1892–1971)

6

Islamic Extremism

"Do not be overcome by evil, but overcome evil with good."
~ Romans 12:21

When it comes to politics in America, what if we actually have more in common that we are led to believe? What if unity could be found not by settling in the middle, but by meeting one another there with humility to practice a politics of compassion that fosters a society grounded in universal concern, care, and compassion for all of its people?

The American philosopher Eric Hoffer was among the most important thinkers of the 20th century. He authored 10 books and was awarded the Presidential Medal of Freedom in 1983. His enduring wisdom came not from the ivory tower, but from his 23 years as a migrant farm worker and longshoreman in California. In the fields and factories, working among the common man, he encountered generosity, civility, and the essence of humankind. It was there that he learned, in his own words, that "Rudeness is the weak man's imitation of strength." As he studied American society and politics, he made this conclusion, which has stood the test of time:

"The game of history is usually played by the best and
the worst
over the heads of the majority in the middle."

Throughout this book, we are reminded that binary thinking—either/or, all or nothing, black and white, left and right—leaves us with only half a mind. So, in this book we are leaving behind all the talking points and soundbytes that dominate our newsfeeds, and applying our understanding of Scripture, centuries of Christian teaching, and our faith experience to the most contentious issues of our time in search of higher truths that lead to more honest and generous conversations.

The issue of global terrorism has, since the events of September 11, 2001, been foremost on the minds of most Americans. According to a recent Gallup poll, "terrorism" is second only to "healthcare" as the most important issue in the 2020 presidential election. Eighty percent of Americans said it was "extremely important or very important."[1]

In this chapter, we are focusing specifically on terrorism associated with Islamic extremism, rather than considering all acts of domestic terrorism. This is primarily due to how the Patriot Act currently defines terrorism. According to the Patriot Act, signed into law on October 26, 2001,

> domestic terrorism is defined as "activities within the US that... involve acts dangerous to human life that... appear to be intended—

> i   to intimidate or coerce a civilian population;

> ii   to influence the policy of a government by intimidation or coercion; or

> iii to affect the conduct of a government by mass destruction, assassination, or kidnapping.

I make this distinction because you may be wondering about the massacre at Mother Emanuel African Methodist Episcopal Church in Charleston that killed nine people, the Orlando Pulse nightclub

---

[1]https://news.gallup.com/poll/276932/several-issues-tie-important-2020-election.aspx

attack that killed 50, or the Las Vegas shooting that killed 59 and injured more than 800. Each of these attacks was perpetrated by non-Muslim American citizens, and any reasonable person would condemn them as acts of terrorism.

According to the Patriot Act, to be legally charged with terrorism, a person must be suspected of acting on behalf of one of 60 groups declared by the State Department as a foreign terrorist organization, including ISIS and al-Qaeda. Most, but not all, of these groups advocate and support Islamic extremism and militant fundamentalism.

Legal definitions aside, the al-Qaeda attacks of September 11, 2001, made terrorism virtually synonymous with Islamist extremism in the minds of most Americans. If there is one belief we all agree on, it's that terrorism is an evil that must be denounced in all of its forms. Where we often disagree politically is on what that means, and the tactics for how to do it.

Throughout this book, we are engaging these contentious issues by using axioms that we can all agree on, despite our partisan differences—statements that are accepted as self-evident and true, regardless of ideological or theological perspectives. Axioms function to establish what is true in order to serve as a starting point for further reasoning. They give us a place to meet and have honest conversations.

Because we are talking about Muslims, it is imperative that we begin with this crucial, if not obvious, first axiom:

Axiom #1: Islam is one of three major monotheistic religions in the world.

Islam is derived from the Old Testament patriarch, Abraham, whom Christians, Jews, and Muslims all claim as the origin of their faith. We all share a common ancestor, Abraham, and a common belief that there is only one God. We all belong to the same family tree.

There are 1.8 billion Muslims in the world—roughly 24 percent of the global population—and 3.45 million Muslims living in the U.S. Islam is the world's second-largest religion, after Christianity, and the fastest-growing religion in the world.

Islam was founded by the Prophet Muhammad, who was born in 570 AD, roughly 540 years after the death of Jesus of Nazareth. He was born in Mecca, on the Arabian Peninsula, which is now Saudi Arabia. At the age of 37, he began secluding himself in a mountain cave named Hira for several nights of prayer. There, he reported being visited by the angel Gabriel in the cave, where he received revelations from God. Three years later, Muhammad started preaching these revelations publicly, proclaiming that "God is One," that complete "submission" (islām) to God is the right course of action (dīn), and that he was a prophet and messenger of God. Gabriel's revelations to Muhammad were transcribed into Islam's central religious text called the Qur'an.

Muhammad's message that "God is One" didn't sit well with his polytheistic audience in Mecca, because Mecca was a major trading hub, and merchants made their living by selling idols. Muhammad's religion was bad for business, and his small group of followers was eventually forced to flee to Medina, about 200 miles to the north. But by 629, Muhammad's followers numbered in the tens of thousands. They marched back to Mecca, seized the city, and by the time of Muhammad's death three years later, most of the Arabian Peninsula had converted to Islam.

The last decade of Muhammad's life was marked by constant "jihad"—or "struggle"—against the enemies of Islam who worshipped many gods. Fighting between tribes became commonplace on the Arabian Peninsula, and it was ultimately through war that Islam defeated the polytheists of Mecca. Muhammad and his followers became known as "valorous warriors," and much of what he taught in this period is about how to fight, as well as the rules of combat. There are about 109 verses in the Qur'an that address fighting and war. The command to "fight" is found only nine times in the Qur'an, and the command to "kill" only five times. But it's these few verses that fuel Islamic extremism and mislead many in the West to believe that Islam as a whole is an inherently violent religion. This leads us to our second axiom:

Axiom #2: Violence is neither a normative behavior nor a core tenant of Islam.

Any mainstream Muslim would describe Islam as a religion of peace, and would sum up their faith practice in "The Five Pillars of Islam:"

- *Shahadah*: reciting the Muslim profession of faith, "There is no God but Allah, and Muhammad is his last messenger."

- *Salat*: praying five times each day

- *Zakat*: charity, or alms-giving, that benefits the poor and the needy

- *Sawm*: fasting during the month of Ramadan

- *Hajj*: pilgrimage to Mecca

Do you see any parallels to our Christian faith: prayer, charity, fasting or self-denial, and the emphasis of spiritual pilgrimage to holy places?

But that is not all we have in common. Jews and Christians share a number of teachings from Scripture that justify and even advocate for violence. If you open your Bible to Deuteronomy, Numbers, or Joshua, you will find countless references to killing the Gentile or anyone who worships other gods, instead of the one God. Take, for example, Deuteronomy 13:6–11

> If anyone secretly entices you—even if it is your brother, your father's son or your mother's son, or your own son or daughter, or the wife you embrace, or your most intimate friend—saying, "Let us go worship other gods," whom neither you nor your ancestors have known, any of the gods of the peoples that are around you, whether near you or far away from you, from one end of the earth to the other, you must not yield to or heed any such persons. Show them no pity or compassion and do not shield them. But you shall surely kill them; your own hand shall be first against them to execute them, and afterwards the hand of all the people. Stone them to death for trying to turn you away from the LORD your God, who brought you

out of the land of Egypt, out of the house of slavery. Then all Israel shall hear and be afraid, and never again do any such wickedness.

This, along with many other similar passages, is actually in our Bible. So how do modern day Jews and Christians interpret these passages? We interpret them through the lens of historical context and modern reason. No reasonable Christian would ever turn a specific scriptural command to kill nonbelieving idol worshippers into a general rule for all time. Time and context have changed; so, too, has our understanding of humankind. Christians would affirm that the teachings of Jesus supersede the Hebraic legal code. In the same way, the vast majority of Muslims today apply a principle called "abrogation" to the Qur'an, which means that a later revelation supersedes a previous one.

Just as we cannot blame all Christians for the evils of the Spanish Inquisition, we cannot blame an entire group of Muslims for the atrocities committed by the few in the name of Islam. We cannot apply the evil of the few to the whole. Every day in the Arab world, Muslims risk and lose their lives in the fight against ISIS and the Taliban. That includes U.S. soldiers who are Muslim.

Because we are commanded in Scripture to avoid "bearing false witness against our neighbor" (Exodus 20:16), it is essential that Christians acknowledge that the overwhelming majority of Muslims are eager to distinguish themselves from the violence of Islamist terrorists. This leads to our third axiom:

Axiom #3: Islamic terrorism emerges not from religion, but from "religion's wicked partner"

—a term coined by the philosopher, William James.

In his classic book, *The Varieties of Religious Experience*, William James distinguishes between the "spirit of religion" and what he called "religion's wicked partner"— "the spirit of dominion."

What is the "spirit of religion?" It is the sense that God exists and is our primary reality, the ground of our being. Out of that sense flows a set of values and practices: prayer, charity for the poor, sacrament, devotion and a genuine desire to grow closer to God. Faith begins with humility before God and a yearning for infinite love.

So, in this sense, the very phrase "Islamic extremism" is flawed because terrorism is not an extension of "the spirit of religion," or of faith. As *New York Times* columnist David Brooks points out, people do not begin with this kind of faith and then naturally turn into terrorists because they become more faithful. Terrorism does not begin with a humble awareness of, or devotion, to God. Terrorism begins with a sense of injury, personal or collective, and a yearning to correct that injury through revenge and domination. It begins with a grievance—that I, or we as a group, have been wronged, and the belief that some external enemy must be responsible.[2]

Only then do the aggrieved reach for religion. You begin with a grievance, an injury, or a hatred, and then you pluck from Scripture whatever verses might help to create an ideology to justify whatever actions will make you feel righteous or heroic. This is not only endemic to Islamic extremism, but to any act of hate carried out in the name of any religion.

Terrorism is an ideology of moral outrage clothed in religious garb. The 9/11 hijackers left behind a trail of drugs, alcohol, gambling, and sexually graphic content in their Florida hotel rooms that is abhorrent to the Muslim religion. The evidence collected after the raid on Osama Bin Laden and his compound revealed similar religious and spiritual contradictions.

It is only when we have a genuine understanding of what religion is and is not that we can form a Christian response to terrorism: by condemning the actions committed in the name of religion instead of condemning an entire group of people who follow that religion; by looking more honestly at the root causes of the grievances that many in the Arab world hold against the West; and by being faithful to the religion inspired by Jesus of Nazareth, which has a lot to say about how we are to live in the face of the enemy. This leads us to our fourth and final axiom:

---

[2]https://www.nytimes.com/2016/06/17/opinion/religions-wicked-neighbor.html

Axiom #4: Only the redeemed can redeem the world.

Friedrich Nietzsche, the German philosopher, once said, "Show me that you are redeemed and then I will believe in your Redeemer." Fear cannot give birth to peace; nor can evil give birth to the justice. Only love can overcome the world; only the redeemed can redeem the world. That is why Paul, writing to the early Christians who endured persecution and violence, said:

> Bless those who persecute you; bless and do not curse them. Rejoice with those who rejoice, weep with those who weep. Live in harmony with one another; do not be haughty, but associate with the lowly; do not claim to be wiser than you are. Do not repay anyone evil for evil, but take thought for what is noble in the sight of all. If it is possible, so far as it depends on you, live peaceably with all. Beloved, never avenge yourselves, but leave room for the wrath of God; for it is written, "Vengeance is mine, I will repay, says the Lord." No, "if your enemies are hungry, feed them; if they are thirsty, give them something to drink; for by doing this you will heap burning coals on their heads." Do not be overcome by evil, but overcome evil with good. (Romans 12:14–21)

We may disagree on policies to address and prevent terrorism on American soil: travel bans, racial profiling, airport security, waterboarding, and Guantanamo Bay. But at the heart of our Christian identity is this radical idea that we can overcome evil with good. We can argue the merits of that strategy on the battlefield, but most of us do not spend our lives on the battlefield. Because we spend most of our lives in our neighborhoods and communities, overcoming evil with good becomes the roadmap to redemption and a prescription for peace.

The majority of non-Muslim Americans today do not know even a single Muslim. Perhaps that is a good place to start with redemption and peacemaking: to form friendships with Muslims, and to lean into those relationships with humility and a desire to learn about the Islamic religion and culture. If we could do that, we would discover that many of our Muslim neighbors in the U.S. live with a chronic sense of fear and mistrust, largely because so many non-Muslims live in fear and mistrust of them. But we are called to live as though we are redeemed by God: fearless, with graciousness, and with gentleness and reverence for the sons and daughters of Abraham, called Muslims, who live among us.

In the 1990s, when violence broke out between ethnic groups in former Yugoslavia, Orthodox Serbians, Croatians, Catholics, and Bosnian Muslims were caught up in a devastating cycle of violence and revenge. In the middle of it all an ecumenical Protestant mission initiative called Agape committed to redeem the brokenness. A Serbian businessman, Antol Bolag, decided to dedicate his life to the promise of God's peace even in the face of ghastly ethnic "cleansing" and interfaith violence. He applied his business skills to an effort to rebuild and resettle Muslim families in villages destroyed by bombs and war. His job was to assemble the raw materials and labor to rebuild the villages, one house at a time.

One day, as he was reviewing reconstruction plans, the village chief asked Bolag why his rebuilding plans included the reconstruction not only of homes, but of the local Muslim mosque. Bolag answered, "We will rebuild your mosque because we follow One who commanded us to love our neighbors as ourselves; one who knelt by the side of the road to minister to a wounded brother without asking him about his theology."[3]

"Do not be overcome by evil, but overcome evil with good." That work starts with acknowledging that our Muslim neighbors share a branch on our religious family tree, which means that we are united by God in kinship; that violence is neither a normative behavior nor a core tenant of Islam, which means that we can surrender our fear of Muslims in favor of finding delight in the beauty of their tradition and practice; that Islamic terrorism emerges not from religion, but from "religion's wicked partner," which permits us to condemn the actions committed in the name of religion without condemning an entire group of people who follow that religion; and that only the redeemed can redeem the world, which calls us once again to a life rooted in kenosis for the sake of the common good.

---

[3]John Buchanan, *A New Church for a New World* (Louisville, KY: Geneva Press, 2008), 79.

Further Study and Reflection for Groups or Individuals

A Prayer for Guidance and Grace

Jesus the Christ, Prince of Peace, you command us to love our enemies and pray for those who persecute us. We pray for our enemies and those who seek to do us harm. By the power of your Holy Spirit, may we all learn to work together for that justice, which brings true and lasting peace. Amen.

Icebreaker

Do you personally have any friends, colleagues, or neighbors who are Muslim? If so, what is important to them? What has been the nature of your interactions or relationships with them?

Do you feel that you have a good understanding of the basic tenets of Islam?

Do you believe that the Islamic religion is more inherently violent than other religions? Why?

Why do you think the issue of terrorism can be such a divisive or contentious issue for Americans?

Are there particular times, places, or experiences that trigger anxiety or fear in you about the possibility of a terrorist attack?

Deep Dive

In what ways is the legal definition of terrorism, as outlined by the Patriot Act, potentially problematic? If the definition of terrorism were to be expanded to include other acts of mass violence not currently addressed in the Patriot Act, what specific acts of terrorism should be included?

What did you learn in this chapter about the history or religion of Islam? What surprised you, concerned you, or resolved your questions or concerns?

How do the "five pillars" of Islam resonate with your own religious experience and practice in the Christian tradition?

What are some of the root causes of the grievances that many Muslims in the Arab world hold against the West and that give rise to an ideology of moral outrage garbed in religious clothing?

With respect to the passages of the Qur'an that encourage violence, the vast majority of Muslims today apply a principle called "abrogation," which means that a later revelation nullifies and supersedes a previous revelation. How do Christians and Jews read similarly problematic, even violent, passages found in the Hebrew and Christian Scriptures?

Engaging the Text

Read Romans 12:17–21.

In what circumstances are you tempted to "repay" someone "evil for evil," and what would it look like if you were to do this?

According to v. 17, what should you do instead of this repaying "evil for evil," and what would that look like?

Are there limits to the extent to which we pursue peace, and if so, what are they and how do we know what they are?

In response to threats or acts of Islamic extremism, what would it look like, personally and practically, for you to "overcome evil with good" (v. 21)?

Closing Prayer

Loving God, have mercy on us and on all that bear us evil will and would do us harm, and on their faults and ours together, by such tender, merciful means, as your infinite wisdom best can devise; grant to amend and redress and make us saved souls in heaven together, where we may ever live and love together with you. And the things, good Lord, that we pray for, give us your grace to labor for. Amen.
~ adapted from St. Thomas More

7

Homosexuality

"When the Spirit of truth comes, he will guide you into all the truth..."
~ John 16:13

"What is to prevent me from being baptized?"
~ Acts 8:37

In February 2019, my denomination, The United Methodist Church, betrayed one of its most essential and enduring rules for Christian practice, which is to "do no harm." At its special General Conference, called specifically to address the issue of same-sex marriage and the ordination of LGBTQ candidates for ministry, The United Methodist Church doubled down on its restrictive policies on homosexuality and, in doing so, did irreparable harm to the LGBTQ community and its allies, as well as to the majority of United Methodists in the U.S. who embrace a more generous orthodoxy and polity. When Christians put archaic rules above real people and the tired laws of man over the timeless love of Christ, the church no longer feels safe—and there are few places in this world where LGBTQ persons do feel safe.

Following the decisions and outcomes of that General Conference in 2019, I was talking to one of the students in my congregation about the implications of these exclusionary policies for our particular church, when it became altogether clear to me that our children and youth will suffer the greatest long-term impact of these policies. A high school freshman, the student shared that he struggles with his faith, like so many kids do, but has found a safe spiritual home in my congregation. His question to me was heartbreaking. He said, "I don't really understand what that vote was all about. But does it mean that some of my friends can't go on the youth mission trip now because they're gay?"

As we address the issue of homosexuality and the Christian faith, I confess at the outset that I dream of a better future for the church. I dream of a day in which the phrase "inclusive church" is a redundancy. I dream of a day in which no gay person has to call the church on Friday to ask if they will be accepted on Sunday. I dream of a day when a sermon about the full inclusion of homosexuals in the life of the church is as incontrovertible as a sermon about renouncing the institution of slavery or granting full and equal rights to all women. That day will come because Jesus proved that the Kingdom comes not only when we take the right stand on issues, but when we dare to stand in the right places, with the right people—the outcasts, the castaways, the rejected, and the marginalized.

Because not all Christians are there yet, we have to acknowledge that, even in our disagreements on this issue, we are still obligated to love one another without conditions, exception, or limitations. John Wesley, who began the movement called Methodism, said, "Though we cannot think alike, may we not love alike? May we not be of one heart, though we are not of one opinion? Without all doubt, we may."

At the heart of the debate for United Methodists is a single phrase, inserted in *The Book of Discipline* in 1972, stating that the "practice of homosexuality is incompatible with Christian teaching." *The Book of Discipline* is the denominational constitution for United Methodists, containing official church law and doctrine. This "incompatibility" clause serves as the basis for specific restrictions: self-avowed, practicing homosexuals are prohibited from ordination and appointment to a local church; pastors are prohibited from officiating at same-sex weddings and are subject to church trial, suspension, and the loss of their credentials for violating this prohibition; and local congregations are prohibited from hosting same-sex weddings on church property.

Whether you are gay or straight, perhaps you are wondering where God is leading you on this issue right now. How can Christians think and talk about homosexuality with honesty, biblical integrity, and genuine compassion?

We are using axioms in this book to help find common ground for the sake of working together for the common good. An axiom is a statement or proposition that is well established or self-evidently true. Our first axiom is taken from a verse of Scripture found in 1 John 4:18:

Axiom #1: "Perfect love casts out fear."

When we talk about homosexuality, we are not talking about an issue; we are talking about us—real people, with real hearts that feel and love like straight people feel and love. For many people who are straight, the issue of homosexuality raises a host of fears and misperceptions that are often overcome only through a relationship with a LGBTQ person, for it is hard to reject someone you have come to know and love.

According to the Pew Research Center, over the last two decades, opinions about same-sex marriage have changed dramatically in the U.S. Today, a majority of Americans (61 percent) favor allowing gays and lesbians to marry legally, while about half as many (31 percent) oppose same-sex marriage. In 2004, the popular opinion was almost the reverse of what it is today: 60 percent opposed same-sex marriage, while just 31 percent were in favor.

Support for same-sex marriage is highest among Millennials (74 percent). A majority of Gen Xers (58 percent) support allowing gays and lesbians to marry legally, as do about half of Baby Boomers (51 percent) and 45 percent of the Silent Generation.[1]

What accounts for this dramatic change in attitudes? Most Americans who have grown in their acceptance of LGBTQ persons

[1] https://www.people-press.org/2019/05/14/majority-of-public-favors-same-sex-marriage-but-divisions-persist/

over the course of their lives have done so, in large part, because they have come to know and love someone who is gay, lesbian, bisexual, or transgender. The more connections Americans made with gay or lesbian people, the more positive their attitudes toward them became—a trend that social scientists call "the contact hypothesis." Christians simply call it the power of radical kinship.

I grew up in a small, decidedly conservative town in Southern California, where the most ubiquitous religious cliché was, "God said it. I believe it. That settles it." I knew that while the Bible did not say much about homosexuality, it did call it an abomination. Because I did not know anyone who was openly gay, I simply accepted the prevailing attitudes and stereotypes of my community and culture. Maybe this is how it was, or is, for you. You do not quite know what you believe, so you accept the views of the status quo.

When I left that little town for college, I met people who were openly gay. From there, I went to seminary and studied alongside gays and lesbians who were not only out and Christian, but who were preparing for ordained ministry. In seminary, I studied the Bible extensively, and my understanding of homosexuality slowly began to evolve. As I studied the verses from Leviticus and Romans that condemn homosexual behavior, I also studied passages from Matthew prohibiting divorce—and thought of my own grandmother who had been divorced twice. I studied passages in the epistles prohibiting women from speaking in church—and yet my own pastor was a woman. I studied the commandment to honor the Sabbath and to keep it holy—even during the NFL season, when the Broncos are playing. I studied passages from Leviticus prohibiting the consumption of pork, fully cognizant that I had eaten bacon for breakfast that week. I studied the life and ministry of Jesus, who loved lepers, Samaritans, the ritually unclean, and outcasts, and after my classes, I would go to work at a county hospital as a phlebotomist, drawing blood from the arms of young men dying from a strange, dreaded disease that marked them as untouchable. I watched their bodies deteriorate over time. I learned their names and their stories. I observed their palpable sense of God-forsakenness and shame.

My understanding of Jesus and Scripture evolved, and I became an ordained minister. I came to know church members who were gay, as well as parents of gay children. They struggled to reconcile their personal experiences with their religious beliefs. Over and over, they would ask me: "Will I be accepted? Will my son be welcomed here?" "Will we be permitted to teach Sunday School?" "Will you baptize our children?"

Perfect love casts out all fear. "Perfect" does not mean flawless or without challenges. In the Greek, the word is "teleia" (τελεία). It means "mature" or "boundless." A mature, boundless love casts out fear, or "phobia" (φόβον)—fear of what we do not understand; fear of rejecting what we have always been taught to believe but do not quite believe anymore; fear of loving like Jesus loved, who was "perfect love" embodied.

A mature, fully developed love persuades us to help people who are hurting, instead of hurting people who are helpless. If we can cast aside the cultural and religious fears that surround this issue, then we can finally dare to read the Bible the way Jesus read his Bible. This leads us to our second axiom:

Axiom #2: Jesus used the whole of Scripture to interpret the individual parts of Scripture.

Bible scholars call this the "principle of unity," and it is akin to ensuring that we see the forest for the trees.

Over and over again, Jesus criticized the religious leaders of his day for picking out the smallest and least important commandments to focus on, while ignoring the weightier matters of faith, such as justice and mercy. He called it "straining out gnats and swallowing camels." "Woe to you... hypocrites! For you tithe mint, dill, and cumin, and have neglected the weightier matters of the law: justice and mercy and faith... You strain out a gnat but swallow a camel!" (Matthew 23:23).

There are about 31,000 verses in the Bible. Only six of those verses reference same-gender sexual relations—of which only three even remotely refer to what today might be considered homosexuality. That is 0.01 percent. That is three trees in a massive forest. Gnats and camels.

How do we see the forest as modern Christians? Biblical scholars speak of what is called "progressive revelation," which suggests that the ways in which God spoke to people in Scripture were understood in light of the concepts, ideas, and assumptions of the times in which the biblical authors lived. Scripture was not dictated by God outside of time and history; it was written by people who were reflecting upon what they understood to be God's will and revelation in their own historical and cultural context. The authors spoke to a particular audience, at a particular time, addressing the particular needs and challenges of their day. Because of this particularity, there is no single verse, or even a small collection of verses, that can fully translate God's revelation for our own time and place. Instead, we have to read these verses within the context of the entire Bible, and especially in light of the life and teachings of Jesus.

When we do that, we begin to see the forest more clearly. We encounter that overwhelming theme that runs throughout the Bible about God's boundless, inexhaustible, and relentless love for all humankind—indeed, all of creation. This love, embodied fully in Christ, sweeps away some highly specific prohibitions. It transcends the law and even religion itself. This boundless love compelled Jesus, in his own time, to announce that the laws and prohibitions of his Jewish religion were no longer relevant to his community. He was asked about divorce, retaliation, adultery, and enemies, and over and over again, he said, "You have heard that it was said long ago... but now I say to you..." (Matthew 5:17–48). What he was saying was, "Love transcends the law." That is the message of Jesus. Real people come before ancient rules. Love transcends the law. Delight in the other supersedes devotion to the institution.

If, like Jesus, you believe that love transcends the law, then your love is no longer constrained by the past. You are free to follow that Spirit of love in your own time. And that leads us to our third axiom:

Axiom #3: God still teaches us through the Holy Spirit.
How did Jesus say it?

I still have many things to say to you, but you cannot bear them now. When the Spirit of truth comes, he will guide you into all the truth; for he will not speak on his own, but will speak whatever he hears, and he will declare to you the things that are to come. He will glorify me, because he will take what is mine and declare it to you. All that the Father has is mine. For this reason I said that he will take what is mine and declare it to you. (John 16:12–15)

What Jesus meant in that moment was that there were things that God still needed to say to us, but we were not able to understand these things at the time. Questions would arise later about particular issues and problems, but it wouldn't make sense to give us the answers to questions we hadn't yet asked. Instead, Jesus had given us a blueprint, and we would have to build the kingdom without him being physically present and based on what we know in the moment. Jesus was suggesting that there would be times when we would wonder what he might have said about this issue or that problem. There were important things that he hadn't spoken about, and we would have questions long after he had left us. So, he would send his Holy Spirit, and his Holy Spirit would dwell in our hearts and remind us of everything that he had said. The Holy Spirit would then explain Jesus' teaching in the light of what is happening in our own time, so that we would know what it means to be a Christian in our world, and how to apply his teachings to the problems before us.

Every time we read the Bible, we have to ask the Holy Spirit what it means and how it applies to our own historical context. If the issue of homosexuality is unresolved for you, invite the Holy Spirit to help you. You can say to the Holy Spirit, "Help me to understand which of your children are a mistake and an abomination in your sight. Help me to understand whom I am supposed to reject, condemn, and exclude in your name, and whom I should accept, welcome, and include."

In Acts 8, a eunuch is traveling from Jerusalem to his home in Ethiopia. He has traveled this great distance to Jerusalem in order to worship there, but the back story is that, because he is a eunuch—because his genitals have been mutilated—he is not permitted to enter the Temple. He is ritually unclean. He is not an outcast. In fact, he is very wealthy. He works for Candace, the Queen of Ethiopia. He's a high-ranking official in the royal court. He is black, which makes him an object of wonder and fascination among the Jews. He is not an outcast, but he is an outsider. He has never been kicked out; he has just never been allowed to come in.

As he's cruising home in his chariot, he reads from the scroll of Isaiah. But he is struggling to understand it. Meanwhile, an evangelist named Philip is waiting by the roadside, having been commanded by an angel to go there and wait. When Philip hears the eunuch reading aloud, he asks him, "Do you understand what that means?" The eunuch says, "How can I, without someone to help me?" Suddenly, we have this tender image of Philip, climbing into the chariot and sharing the gospel of Jesus Christ with a eunuch, an outsider, who longs to know the love of God.

But the most powerful scene in this story occurs when the eunuch rolls down the window of his chariot limousine and spots a pond. He asks his chauffeur to pull over and stop the car, and he asks Philip, "Is there anything that prevents me from being baptized right now? Is there any rule that says a eunuch like me can't be baptized?"

This outsider who, because of some bizarre law about genitalia is prevented from worshiping in the temple, is asking Philip, "Can I be included? Is there anything that prevents me from being a part of the Christian community?"

Philip doesn't say, "Hold on while I check *The Book of Discipline*." He doesn't call headquarters to speak with the bishop first. He just says, "Get in the water." And when the eunuch steps into the waters of his baptism, suddenly his whole life story changes. He is no longer looking in from the outside. He is included in God's boundless love. For once in his life, he belongs.

This happened because Philip asked the Holy Spirit: "Holy Spirit, help me to see who ought to be excluded and who ought to be included."

Two hundred years ago, the church said that slavery was biblically justified. It said, "Don't mix politics and religion. Just preserve the status quo. It's in the Bible." But John Wesley heard the Holy Spirit, and spoke up: "Give liberty to whom liberty is due—to every partaker of human nature. Away with all whips, all chains, all compulsion. Be gentle toward all."[2]

For centuries, the Church said that women shouldn't speak in church, and couldn't be ordained. It's in the Bible. It wasn't until 1956 that Methodists heard the voice of the Holy Spirit—although Wesley, 200 years earlier, had spoken clearly on the issue: "It has long passed for a maxim... that 'women are only to be seen but not heard'... No, it is the deepest unkindness; it is horrid cruelty; it is barbarity. And I know not how any women of sense and spirit can submit to it."[3] Yet many other Christian denominations (and other religions) still exclude women from leadership.

What Wesley was saying was this: Perfect love casts out fear. Love transcends the law. God is still speaking.

Further Study and Reflection for Groups or Individuals

A Prayer for Guidance and Grace

Creator God, you have made all things beautifully and in your divine image. As we lift up the diversity of your creation, teach us to love fully and radically all of your children, as their true and whole selves, and empower us to resist evil, injustice, and oppression in whatever forms they present themselves. Amen.

Icebreaker

Over the course of your life, have you personally grown in your understanding and acceptance of LGBTQ persons? If so, how and why?

Do you have a close friend or family member who is openly LGBTQ? How has your friendship with them changed/not changed your acceptance of LGBTQ people?

---

[2]Excerpt from the 1774 pamphlet "Thoughts upon Slavery"

[3]Paul Wesley Chilcote, *Wesley Speaks on Christian Vocation* (Eugene, OR: Wipf and Stock Publishers, 2001), 58.

Does acceptance of homosexuality conflict with your religious beliefs or your understanding of the Bible? If not now, has it in the past? (How) have you reconciled this conflict?

Deep Dive

What accounts for the dramatic change in the attitudes of Americans over the last decade regarding LGBTQ persons and same sex marriage?

How did Jesus, in his own historical context, use the whole of Scripture to interpret the individual parts of Scripture?

What do Bible scholars mean by the phrase "progressive revelation," and how does this apply to how we read the Bible in modern times?

What is the role of the Holy Spirit in discerning the will of God on problematic issues?

Engaging the Text

Read Acts 8:26–39.

What is a eunuch, and why were eunuchs excluded from the temple?

What challenges, if any, did Philip have to overcome—social, cultural, religious, or otherwise—in order to relate to the eunuch?

What was the eunuch asking or searching for?

How did God use Philip to minister to the Eunuch?

What does this passage teach us about the rules and prohibitions of religious tradition?

Closing Prayer

Let nothing disturb you, Let nothing frighten you,
All things are passing away:
God never changes.
Patience obtains all things
Whoever has God lacks nothing; God alone suffices.
~ Teresa of Avila (1515–1582)

8

Social Isolation and Suicide

"A man ran up and knelt before him, and asked him,
"Good Teacher, what must I do to inherit eternal life?""
~ Mark 10:17

Somewhere in the North Pacific Ocean right now is a whale that has come to be known simply as "52." Scientists have been tracking 52 for 30 years, but nobody has actually seen him. They know that 52 is a male because he vocalizes during mating season like only male whales do. But his species is uncertain. He might be a fin whale, or a blue whale. Nobody knows for sure because his mating call doesn't match the frequency of any other species of whale in the world.

Whale 52 gets his name from his unique sonic signature. He vocalizes at a frequency of 52 hertz. Fin whales vocalize at 20 hertz; blue whales between 10 and 39 hertz. But 52 has this grating, high-pitched voice that makes him sound like the Mickey Mouse or the Mike Tyson of the underwater world. And it's because of that annoying voice that 52 has spent his entire life alone. He has roamed the world's largest ocean for years, singing his forlorn love songs, desperately crying out for a mate—but never finding one.

Over the years, 52 has become known as "The World's Loneliest Whale." He has become a worldwide celebrity, a cultural icon, and a symbol for the feelings of scores of lonely, disconnected people around the world. This profoundly social, communal creature that can feel love, pain, grief, and empathy has become a symbol for every human being who has ever longed for relationship, community, and belonging but has never found it.

According to social scientists, we are the loneliest generation in American history, living in an unprecedented era of social isolation. The great paradox of the digital age is that, despite the virtual connectivity of Facebook, Instagram, and Twitter, we have never been more disconnected from one another—and we have never been unhappier. This is not a uniquely American phenomenon. In February 2018, Prime Minister Theresa May appointed Tracey Crouch to serve as the world's first "Minister of Loneliness" in the UK—to address what May called the "sad reality of modern life."

In America, the statistics are startling:

- One in four Americans (27 percent) rarely or never feels as though there are people who really understand them.

- Nearly five out of ten Americans (46 percent) report feeling always or sometimes lonely.

- One in five Americans (20 percent) reports they rarely or never feel close to people or feel like they have people they can talk to (18 percent).

- Only around half of Americans (53 percent) have meaningful in-person social interactions, such as having an extended conversation with a friend or spending quality time with family, on a daily basis.

- Generation Z (those born between 1995 and 2012) is the loneliest generation.[1]

What is loneliness? It is the subjective perception that we lack belonging and connection in our lives. There is no "loneliness"

---

[1]https://www.cigna.com/newsroom/news-releases/2018/new-cigna-study-reveals-loneliness-at-epidemic-levels-in-america

test. If a person thinks they are lonely, then they are lonely. People can be lonely while in solitude, or in the middle of a crowd. What makes a person lonely is that they need more social interaction or a certain type of social interaction than is currently available. In the last 50 years, the rate of loneliness has doubled in the United States.

What is going on in our world that is making us feel lonelier and more disconnected from one another?

Sociologist Brené Brown suggests that at the heart of the problem is "social sorting." "We are more sorted than we have ever been in the history of the U.S." says Brown. We have built ideological bunkers. We are more likely now to live with, worship with, and go to school with people who are politically and ideologically likeminded."[2] In other words, we associate with people who think, believe, and look like us—and we have little interest in people who are not like us. This makes it easier for us to turn away from one another and toward blame and outrage. As we try to protect our cherished beliefs, we either withdraw and keep quiet, or we pick sides and adopt the behavior of the people with whom we passionately disagree.

So the correlation is not coincidental: the more socially sorted we are, the lonelier we become. The more walls we build to protect ourselves, the more isolated we become. The less time we spend with those who are not like us, the less at home we are with ourselves.

In the Gospel of Mark, a man comes to Jesus one day with an urgent question. He wants to know what he must do to inherit eternal life. He is a wealthy man, but this story is not primarily about his wealth. He has earned his wealth by honest means. He has lived a good life. He has always been very religious, saying his prayers, following the commandments, reading his Bible, and going to church.

But something is missing in his life.

---

[2]https://www.cbsnews.com/news/author-brene-brown-social-scientist-new-book-braving-the-wilderness/

"Jesus," he says, "is there anything else that I must do to gain eternal life?"

Jesus looks on him with deep love. He knows he is a good man, but that he is lonely. He knows that what this good man needs most is nothing less than a matter of life and death.

"There is just one thing left to do," he tells the man. "Go sell whatever you own and give it to the poor."

But this is the last thing the man expected to hear, and he walks off with a heavy heart. Alone.

This is not primarily a story about wealth. If all we have to do to gain eternal life is to give away our stuff, we would all do that— eventually. But God is not a vending machine. We cannot drop our quarters in a slot and expect God to dispense a serving of life everlasting.

What we have is a story about a man whose wealth and religion have become an obstacle to building meaningful, deep connections with the people around him. His wealth and his religion have sorted him right out of human community. He wants to know how to get to eternity, and Jesus turns him around and tells him that the way to eternity is through the temporal. He comes to Jesus alone, and Jesus turns him around and points him back to his neighbors, to the people to whom he truly belongs but does not know. It is not the giving away of his possessions that will save him; it is the giving of himself to his community—this is what will cure his deep heart sickness, his palpable loneliness.

The mystic poet, William Blake, put it this way: "Eternity is in love with the creations of time."

If eternity is what you long for, then love what eternity loves: the creations of time, including people, community, human connection. This, according to Jesus, is our salvation: connection, and belonging.

Humans are not wired to be alone. We first evolved on the savannas of Africa, where we lived in small hunter-gatherer tribes of a few hundred people. You and I exist in large part because our ancestors learned how to live together by fostering the communal values of cooperation and reciprocal commitment. They were able to take down large animals together. They shared their bananas and nursed their sick. Individual survival was made possible only by remaining connected to the tribe. If, on those savannas, you became separated from the tribe and were alone for any length of time, it meant that you were in grave danger. You were vulnerable to predators, illness, and starvation. Should you become separated from your tribe, the fear of being alone would shoot cortisol through your veins. Your anxiety would rise, and that anxiety would send an urgent signal to your brain to find any way necessary to get back to the tribe.[3]

For our earliest ancestors, that anxiety was a healthy trigger that compelled them to get back to their tribe. But today, that trigger is not working. We medicate it. We numb it. We suppress and divert it. We replace real human connection with digital "friends" or "followers." That anxiety of being alone has nowhere to go, except to our hearts and minds, where it aches. We are not only the loneliest generation in history, but also the most anxious and depressed—which accounts, in large part, for why we are killing ourselves at an unprecedented rate.

According to the American Psychological Association, the suicide rate increased 33 percent from 1999 through 2017, from 10.5 to 14 suicides per 100,000 people. Rates have increased more sharply since 2006. Suicide ranks as the fourth leading cause of death for people ages 35 to 54, and the second for 10 to 34-year-olds. It remains the 10th leading cause of death in the U.S. overall.[4]

In 2017, 1,400,000 Americans attempted suicide, and 47,173 Americans died by suicide—an average of 129 suicides per day. The demographic most vulnerable to suicide is white men, ages 35 to 54. Males are 3.5 times more likely to take their own lives than

---

[3]See Johann Hari, *Lost Connections: Uncovering the Real Causes of Depression – and the Unexpected Solutions* (London: Bloomsbury Publishing, 2018). Kindle Edition, 77–79.

[4]https://www.apa.org/monitor/2019/03/trends-suicide

women, accounting for 70 percent of all suicides.[5] Suicide among girls and women between 2000 and 2016 is up 50 percent.[6]

Some of the major risk factors for suicide include: a family history of suicide, clinical depression and anxiety, alcohol or substance abuse, a feeling of hopelessness, or a significant loss, such as the loss of a job, a relationship, or financial security.

Risk factors for suicide among youth include all of these, as well as bullying and social rejection, the pressure to achieve academically, and struggles with sexual orientation. Thus, LGBTQ youth are almost five times more likely to attempt suicide than their straight peers.[7]

Suicide is a complex issue, and the more we oversimplify it, the less equipped we are to prevent it, and the more we lose touch with the people who have been deeply affected by it. Every suicide intimately impacts at least six people[8]—people who belong to the so-called "kinship of survivors." If you are reading this chapter, there is a good chance that you are a member of that kinship of survivors.

As a pastor, I have buried too many people who have ended their own lives. I have taken calls at all hours of the day and night from people planning their suicide, and calls from those who had just attempted suicide only to experience a moment of regret and panic. I have sat with them in emergency rooms and behavioral health units, and I have sat with parents, friends, siblings, and colleagues in hospitals and mortuaries grieving the deaths of loved ones who had ended their lives.

As we explore the difficult and tender issue of suicide, we will begin with what we, as people of faith, can all affirm:

---

[5]https://afsp.org/about-suicide/suicide-statistics/
[6]https://www.apa.org/monitor/2019/01/numbers
[7]https://www.thetrevorproject.org/resources/preventing-suicide/facts-about-suicide/
[8]https://www.health.harvard.edu/mind-and-mood/left-behind-after-suicide

Axiom #1: We are so much more than the worst thing we have ever done.

We are more than the worst thing we have ever done, and that applies even when the worst thing someone has ever done is the last they have ever done.

It is a terrible tragedy when someone takes his or her own life; but a second tragedy occurs when the shame and stigma that is so often associated with suicide prevents the survivors from the healing that can only be found in a community free of judgment and condemnation. When people take their lives, there are often two deaths: the physical death of a loved one, and the social deaths of the survivors who are overwhelmed by stigma, shame, and secrecy.

Years ago, I was called to officiate at a funeral for a 24-year-old man. The immigrant family needed a pastor. They explained that their son had been sick for many years, but they did not elaborate. In broken English they said, "We are Catholic, but the priest is not available."

Days later, we gathered for the service. As several people came to the podium to speak, one of the friends stood up and said to the crowd, "Even though Miguel took his own life, I believe he's in heaven now."

After the service I asked the family, "Were you afraid to tell me?" The mother said, "Pastor, in our culture, suicide is called 'the unforgivable sin of Judas.' We were afraid that our priest would refuse to give us a funeral mass."

We are so much more than the worst thing we have ever done, and that is true even when the worst thing someone could ever do is the last they do.

Nowhere in Scripture is suicide referred to as "the sin of Judas" or an unforgivable sin. There is no divine condemnation of those who take their lives. There is only profound divine grief and sadness. There is divine disappointment, because the God who began a good work in that person was unable to complete it, and that brings God grief. But God's mercy is God's only justice. God is a God of grace for those with broken minds or broken hearts, for the weary and heavy-laden. Recall the Apostle Paul's assurance: "I am convinced that neither death, nor life, nor angels, nor rulers, nor things present, nor things to come, nor powers, nor height, nor depth, nor anything else in all creation, will be able to separate us from the love of God" (Romans 8:38–39).

Because we are all more than the worst thing we have ever done, we can forgive those who die by suicide, as God has forgiven them. Grace for the victims of suicide is a divine choice. Grace for ourselves as we grieve the loss of a loved one to suicide is essential. This leads us to our second axiom:

Axiom #2: Suicide is preventable, but our personal power to prevent others from taking their own lives is finite.

Surviving family and friends commonly suffer from feelings of extreme guilt for not being able to prevent the suicide. They feel a sense of failure because the person they loved felt unloved. They inevitably hear that voice of guilt telling them that they could have done more: "If only I had paid attention... If only I hadn't left the room... If only I had stayed on the phone... If only I had done more." But our personal power to prevent others from taking their lives is finite. There are limits to what we can do.

The Golden Gate Bridge in San Francisco is the most popular suicide site in the world. Since it was built in the 1930s, about 2,000 people have leapt to their deaths from it. The city employs full-time, around-the-clock "Bridgewatch Angels" to patrol the bridge. Their job is to stop people from jumping. They are trained to look for physical signs in pedestrians, to counsel would-be jumpers. They save lives every day. But despite all of their training and vigilance, there are still about 30 people a year who jump to their deaths. The Bridgewatch Angels will tell you, "We simply can't stop them all."

In a world of infinite possibilities, we will always feel like we can do more. But also in this world of infinite possibilities, we are still finite creatures. So, we have to have grace with ourselves. We have to accept what we cannot control. We cannot stop them all.

In a similar manner, even Jesus could not prevent the death of everyone. When Jesus learned of the death of his friend, Lazarus, he wept. People said, "Why didn't you come sooner? Had you been here, you could have prevented this." In a moment of raw humanity, Jesus shed real tears.

Whenever there is a suicide, we can imagine that there may have been more that could have been done. But that does not mean that we could have done more. Those who take their lives play a decisive role in their deaths—most often independent of our efforts or knowledge. This leads us to our third axiom:

Axiom #3: Suicide is a permanent solution to a temporary problem.

For those who struggle with depression, it is imperative to remember that mental illness is not one's identity. Depression and anxiety are not who a person is; it is something a person has. Who we are is God's beloved, and God takes delight in us. We have some degree of human agency in our wellness. No one can make that choice for us.

We know that 80 to 90 percent of people who seek treatment for depression are treated successfully through the use of therapy and/or medication.[9] Depression can be successfully treated, but only half of all Americans experiencing major depression receive treatment. You have to make that choice.

I know many people who have attempted suicide and failed. After finding treatment, what they have told me, without exception, is how thankful they are that their suicide attempt was not successful.

A 1978 study tracked 515 people who were stopped from jumping off the Golden Gate Bridge. Decades later, 94 percent of those

---

[9]https://www.psychiatry.org/patients-families/depression/what-is-depression

people were still alive or had died of natural causes. They lived because they found help.[10]

Over and over again we have to be reminded that it can get better—not because life just naturally gets better, but because we can choose to make it better. We have to make that choice, and when we do, the overwhelming data says it will get better. So, we owe it to our future to live—to refuse to allow the impulse of the moment to dictate the judgment of future decades. Suicide is a permanent solution to a temporary problem. We owe it to our future to live.

The overwhelming majority of those who survive a suicide attempt report immediate regret about the act itself. Kevin Hines is one of only 26 people to have jumped from the Golden Gate Bridge and survived, plummeting 220 ft. into San Francisco Bay and hitting the water at 75 miles per hour. He said that as soon as his hands left the bridge's railing, he thought to himself, "I don't want to die."[11] This leads us to our fourth and final axiom:

Axiom #4: The worst thing that has happened to you does not have to be the last thing.

This is especially meant for those who do not necessarily struggle with clinical depression but who, in the face of disappointment, failure, betrayal, or bullying, feel that they will never get through it. The worst thing that has happened to you doesn't have to be the last thing.

We know that not all suicides are a consequence of clinical depression. Sometimes, suicide is the tragic outcome of a reflexive, impulsive action that a person would regret moments later, if given the chance. This is especially true for young people, who do not have a fully formed prefrontal cortex and the life experience to recognize that they will get through their worst moment.

One of the risk factors for teen suicide is the overwhelming pressure for academic achievement. When you talk to teens, they

---

[10]https://www.latimes.com/opinion/la-xpm-2012-may-25-la-oe-adv-bateson-golden-gate-20120525-story.html

[11]http://content.time.com/time/nation/article/0,8599,1197685,00.html

will tell you that the number one struggle in their lives is stress over grades and test scores. They feel like every decision, every action, every test, is of enormous consequence that will affect the course of their lives forever. When they experience failure, or fall short of their expectations or the expectations of others, they lack the emotional resilience, the life experience, and the fully developed prefrontal cortex to keep life in perspective.

There is an indisputable correlation between teen suicide and the pressure to achieve and succeed. So we have say to our children and to our students: you are not the sum of your achievements or your failures. Your test scores are not your identity; your GPA will not determine your future. You will make mistakes and you will experience failure, but you will always have the opportunity to redeem yourself. It is never too late to begin again.

What about the rest of us? Maybe you have never suffered from suicidal ideation, or struggled to hold on in the face of overwhelming hardship. Maybe you have never experienced a suicide in your family or circle of friends. Where does that leave you?

You have a choice, too—and it is a choice that can make all the difference. The well-being of the community is only made possible by people like you who practice the generous love of Jesus. You can save a life—most likely not in some heroic "extraordinary measure" kind of way, like the good people patrolling the Golden Gate Bridge. But in everyday, ordinary ways.

As the great spiritual writer, Ram Dass, once said, "We're all just walking each other home." So, commit to walking with someone. Share the road in radical kinship with those who walk alone. More than half of our neighbors report that they are lonely. Too many of them are trying to walk home alone, and they never get there. With whom are you walking?

Our mission is simply to come alongside those who are walking alone, and to infuse them with our lives, compassion, and presence. A life rooted in kenosis calls us to pour out our spirit into others— freely, generously, compassionately. That infusion can save a life. It can resuscitate a community. It can restore us to our tribe, where we can finally find a home in the delight of others.